Honey Bunny

AMIGURUMI DRESS-UP DOLL
WITH GARDEN PLAY MAT

Honey Bunny

AMIGURUMI DRESS-UP DOLL
WITH GARDEN PLAY MAT

CROCHET PATTERNS FOR BUNNY DOLL plus
DOLL CLOTHES, GARDEN PLAYMAT & ACCESSORIES

Linda Wright

Dedicated to my inspirations for this book: my sister-in-law, Bunny;
my grandnieces, Staley and Byrne; and my house-rabbit, Homer.

Also by Linda Wright

Amigurumi Toilet Paper Covers
Amigurumi Golf Club Covers
Amigurumi Animal Hats
Amigurumi Animal Hats Growing Up
Amigurumi Animal Hats for 18-Inch Dolls
Amigurumi Holiday Hats for 18-Inch Dolls
Toilet Paper Origami
Toilet Paper Origami On a Roll

Acknowledgements

Afghan on Page 2 by Dolores Wright

Lindaloo Enterprises
P.O. Box 90135
Santa Barbara, California 93190
United States
sales@lindaloo.com

ISBN: 978-1-937564-13-1
Library of Congress Control Number: 2019900049

CONTENTS

INTRODUCTION

Welcome to Honey Bunny's world of fun, creative play and learning about gardening along the way! Honey Bunny is a sweet 10" soft bunny that is a nice size to hold in your hand. Besides the bunny, you will find patterns in this book for a wardrobe of charming girl-bunny and boy-bunny clothes plus a magnificent plant-and-pick Garden Playmat. You will also find patterns for garden tools, Honey Bunny's garden friends and a carrot-shaped sleeping bag to tuck your bunny into at bedtime.

These projects were designed to be cute—and also easy—so that even a novice crocheter can complete the patterns with success. Before starting, be sure to read through the next two introductory pages plus the Stitches and Techniques sections at the back of the book for helpful tips.

If you're new to crocheting and like to learn by watching, YouTube.com offers a treasure trove of excellent crocheting tutorials. I have assembled a collection of my favorites on Pinterest. You can view them at www.pinterest.com/LindalooEnt/ on a board named "Amigurumi Tutorials". There you can see video demos for the stitches and techniques used in these patterns. You will also see some of my favorite products.

Amigurumi is a Japanese word for crocheted animals, dolls and toys. It primarily uses the single crochet stitch plus a lot of working in the round. Amigurumi is meant to be crocheted rather tightly. This prevents fiberfill from showing through the stitches on stuffed pieces. It is also standard procedure in amigurumi to leave a long tail when fastening off. The tail comes in handy when multiple pieces must be sewn together. Sewing thread can also be used for this purpose. Color is a huge aspect of amigurumi and you can have fun using your yarn stash to make the little items in Honey Bunny's wardrobe in lots of different colors.

You will find it easiest to dress your bunny by sliding the clothes on feet-first. If your bunny is made for display, not for play, you can add wire inside the arms, legs or both so that it will hold a pose. (See "Adding Wire" on page 64.) Even without wire, the bunny has been designed to sit nicely.

This book uses U.S. crochet terms. If an instruction says sc, that is a U.S. single crochet—or a U.K. double crochet. Please refer to the stitch diagrams at the back of the book to be sure you are making the stitches as intended.

Designing these patterns was a true joy, taking me back to my days of childhood play. I hope that all who crochet these items, and those who play with them, will enjoy them just as much! Let's hop to it!

♥ Linda

Supplies

Yarn

These projects have been made with soft acrylic yarns that are readily available, inexpensive and washable. Soft yarns frequently include "soft" in their name. Worsted-weight yarn is used when a sturdy structure is desired while DK/Light Worsted is used for items that need drape or a more delicate nature. Be sure to refer to each pattern for its yarn weight specification. I have used various brands and you will find my choices listed in the Resources section at the back of the book.

Crochet Hook

The following hooks are used: F5/3.75mm, G6/4mm and H8/5mm. My favorite hook is the Clover Soft Touch. I love the thick handle and the shape of the head which inserts easily into a stitch.

Yarn Needle

You will need a large-eyed needle to sew the various pieces of your items together and also to finish them off by weaving the loose ends into your work. Yarn needles with a blunt point are readily available. These will do the job though the blunt point tends to catch on the yarn and require some wiggling to push it through. I much prefer a needle with a sharp point. My favorite needle for sewing amigurumi is the Size 14 Chenille or Embroidery needle. These needles can be hard to find in stores, but they are available for purchase online.

Stitch Markers

Stitch markers are used to keep track of where a round or row of crochet begins and ends. You can use a bobby pin, safety pin or purchased stitch markers. You can also use a scrap of yarn (see page 63). Making the correct number of stitches is important, so count to double check if ever you're not sure.

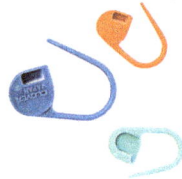

Animal Eyes

Plastic animal safety eyes can be purchased at craft stores or online. A list of internet sources is included in my Resources section at the back of the book. Each eye has a post section and a washer. To attach, work post into a gap between stitches. Place washer against post, lay eye against a hard surface and press washer firmly.

Straight Pins

Use standard dressmaker's pins or long corsage pins to hold pieces in place before sewing.

Ruler

For measuring and marking.

Sewing Needle & Thread

You will need these sewing box basics.

Row Counter

Well worth the investment, a row counter keeps track of what round or row of the pattern you are crocheting. A pencil and paper can also be used.

Removable Notes

Use small sticky notes to keep track of your place in a pattern. Every time you complete a round or a row, move the note down to reveal the next line of instructions.

Scissors

You will need a small pair of sharp scissors.

Stuffing

It can be tricky to know when to stuff an amigurumi. I prefer waiting until I'm done crocheting a piece; otherwise, I'm constantly struggling to keep the stuffing from tangling in my hook. The eraser end of a new pencil, a blunt-tipped chopstick or 6-inch tweezers make great stuffing tools. I especially love my straight-tip serrated tweezers for small pieces. Using them, I can easily insert a wad of stuffing through a tiny opening—even through the space between stitches! Polyester fiberfill is the best stuffing material. Yarn scraps can be used for stuffing small pieces.

Hook & Loop Fastener Tape

Sew-on hook and loop fastener tape is used to attach several of the vegetables to the garden. Be sure to get the sew-on type because it is also sold with a sticky back and that kind is very difficult to sew through. Even the sew-on hook and loop fastener tape is tough stuff and a thimble will help when sewing it by hand. While most retail packaging includes both sides (hook and loop), business products are usually sold separately. I like purchasing them separately so I can get brown hook tape (rough side) for the "dirt" portion of the garden, plus green and orange loop tape (soft side) for the veggies. For my source, see page 65.

Abbreviations

The following abbreviations are used:

yd = yard

st = stitch

ch = chain

sc = single crochet

hdc = half double crochet

dc = double crochet

tr = triple or treble crochet

sl st = slip stitch

rnd = round

sc2tog = single crochet 2 stitches together

dc2tog = double crochet 2 stitches together

* * = a set of stitches

( ) = stitch count

Gauge

Gauge is a measure of how big your stitches are. It's very common for gauge to vary from person to person because not all crocheters stitch the same way. Yarn selection also affects gauge. Some yarns are thinner than others despite being in the same weight category. To alter your gauge, adjust your crochet tension (tightness); change to a larger or smaller crochet hook; try a different brand of hook; or try a different brand of yarn. The following gauge is used in these patterns.

With **G6/4mm hook** and **DK, Light Worsted yarn**:

20 sc = 4"

25 rows = 4"

With **G6/4mm hook** and **Worsted Weight yarn**:

19 sc = 4"

22 rows = 4"

How to Read a Pattern

Each round or row is written on a new line. Most rounds have a repeated section of instructions that are written between two asterisks *like this*. The instruction between the asterisks is to be repeated as many times as indicated before you move on to the next step. At the end of a round, the total number of stitches to be made in that round is indicated in parentheses (like this).

Let's look at a round from the bunny.

Rnd 6: *sc in next 4 sts, 2 sc in next st* 6 times (36 sts).

This means:

Rnd 6	This is the 6th round of the pattern.
sc in next 4 sts	Make 1 single crochet stitch in each of the next 4 stitches
2 sc in next st	Make 2 single crochet stitches, both in the same stitch
6 times	Repeat everything between * and * 6 times.
(36 sts)	The round will have a total of 36 stitches.

So, following the instructions for Round 6, you will:

single crochet in the next 4 sts, 2 sc in the next st,
single crochet in the next 4 sts, 2 sc in the next st,
single crochet in the next 4 sts, 2 sc in the next st,
single crochet in the next 4 sts, 2 sc in the next st,
single crochet in the next 4 sts, 2 sc in the next st,
single crochet in the next 4 sts, 2 sc in the next st,

for a total of 36 stitches.

Honey Bunny

Honey Bunny is made of worsted-weight yarn for a sturdy structure. The bunny will still be soft and cuddly! Honey-colored yarn is used here and Lion Brand "Heartland" is an excellent choice. This is a heathered yarn which creates complexity in the color and a multi-dimensional look. The color I used is called "Great Sand Dunes" and there are many other colors in the Heartland collection that would make lovely bunnies.

All parts are crocheted as a continuous spiral by working in the round. When crocheting small cylinders such as the arms and legs, a running stitch marker is ideal (see page 63). The eraser end of a new pencil makes a great stuffing tool: By twisting the pencil as you push, the eraser will grab the stuffing nicely.

SIZE

10" tall, not including ears

SUPPLIES

G6/4mm crochet hook

110 yds of Worsted weight yarn

2 black animal eyes, 8mm

1 black animal eye, 6mm

Stuffing

MEDIUM 4

HEAD

Make a magic ring, ch 1.

Rnd 1: 6 sc in ring, pull ring closed tight (6 sts).

Rnd 2: 2 sc in each st around. Place marker for beginning of rnd and move marker up as each rnd is completed (12 sts).

Rnd 3: *sc in next st, 2 sc in next st* 6 times (18 sts).

Rnd 4: *sc in next 2 sts, 2 sc in next st* 6 times (24 sts).

Rnd 5: *sc in next 3 sts, 2 sc in next st* 6 times (30 sts).

Rnd 6: *sc in next 4 sts, 2 sc in next st* 6 times (36 sts).

Rnd 7: sc in each st around.

Rnd 8: *sc in next 5 sts, 2 sc in next st* 6 times (42 sts).

Rnds 9-13: sc in each st around.

Rnd 14: *sc in next 5 sts, sc2tog* 6 times (36 sts).

Rnd 15: *sc in next 4 sts, sc2tog* 6 times (30 sts).

Rnd 16: *sc in next 3 sts, sc2tog* 6 times (24 sts).

Rnd 17: *sc in next 2 sts, sc2tog* 6 times (18 sts).

Rnd 18: *sc in next st, sc2tog* 6 times (12 sts).

Sl st in next st. Fasten off.

Stuff head half way; attach eyes (8mm) in groove between Rnds 12-13 spaced 1 1/2" apart. The remaining animal eye (6mm) is used for the bunny's nose. Attach this in groove between Rnds 14-15. Finish stuffing head.

BODY

Make a magic ring, ch 1.

Rnd 1: 6 sc in ring, pull ring closed tight (6 sts).

Rnd 2: 2 sc in each st around. Place marker for beginning of rnd and move marker up as each rnd is completed (12 sts).

Rnd 3: *sc in next st, 2 sc in next st* 6 times (18 sts).

Rnd 4: *sc in next 2 sts, 2 sc in next st* 6 times (24 sts).

Rnd 5: *sc in next 3 sts, 2 sc in next st* 6 times (30 sts).

Rnd 6: *sc in next 9 sts, 2 sc in next st* 3 times (33 sts).

Rnds 7-14: sc in each st around.

Rnd 15: *sc in next 9 sts, sc2tog* 3 times (30 sts).

Rnd 16: *sc in next 3 sts, sc2tog* 6 times (24 sts).

Rnd 17: *sc in next 6 sts, sc2tog* 3 times (21 sts).

Rnd 18: *sc in next 5 sts, sc2tog* 3 times (18 sts).

Rnd 19: *sc in next 4 sts, sc2tog* 3 times (15 sts).

Rnd 20: *sc in next 3 sts, sc2tog* 3 times (12 sts).

Sl st in next st. Fasten off.

Stuff body. Sew head and body together, packing in more stuffing at the junction when seam is nearly closed to add more neck support.

LEG (MAKE 2)

Make a magic ring, ch 1.

Rnd 1: 6 sc in ring, pull ring closed tight (6 sts).

Rnd 2: 2 sc in each st around. Place marker for beginning of rnd and move marker up as each rnd is completed (12 sts).

Rnd 3: *sc in next st, 2 sc in next st* 6 times (18 sts).

Rnd 4: sc in each st around.

Rnd 5: sc2tog 3 times, sc in next 12 sts (15 sts).

Rnd 6: sc2tog 3 times, sc in next 9 sts (12 sts).

Rnd 7: sc2tog twice, sc in next 8 sts (10 sts).

Rnd 8: sc2tog twice, sc in next 6 sts (8 sts).

Rnds 9-18: sc in each st around. Push in stuffing with eraser end of new pencil stuffing lightly in last 4 rnds.

Row 19: With front of foot facing you, flatten open end, ch 1, sc in each st across working through all layers to close top of leg (4 sts).

Fasten off. Sew legs to body on Rnds 1-4 (see photo next page).

ARM (MAKE 2)

Make a magic ring, ch 1.

Rnd 1: 8 sc in ring, pull ring closed tight (8 sts).

Rnds 2-3: sc in each st around. Place marker for beginning of rnd and move marker up as each rnd is completed.

Rnd 4: sc2tog twice, sc in next 4 sts (6 sts).

Rnds 5-18: sc in each st around.

Sl st in next st. Fasten off. With eraser end of new pencil, push stuffing into hand only; do not stuff arm.

Sew an arm to each side where head meets body.

EAR (MAKE 2)

Make a magic ring, ch 1.

Rnd 1: 6 sc in ring, pull ring closed tight (6 sts).

Rnd 2: *sc in next st, 2 sc in next st* 3 times (9 sts).

Rnd 3: *sc in next 2 sts, 2 sc in next st* 3 times (12 sts).

Rnd 4: *sc in next 3 sts, 2 sc in next st* 3 times (15 sts).

Rnds 5-12: sc in each st around.

Fasten off. Flatten ear and sew bottom edges together. Fold ear in half lengthwise so that lower corners meet. Sew a stitch to fasten corners together.

Sew ears close together at top of head. Pinch tips to make nice points.

TAIL

Make a magic ring, ch 1.

Rnd 1: 6 sc in ring, pull ring closed tight (6 sts).

Rnd 2: 2 sc in each st around. Place marker for beginning of rnd and move marker up as each rnd is completed (12 sts).

Rnd 3: sc in each st around.

Rnd 4: sc2tog 6 times (6 sts).

Sl st in next st. Fasten off.

Stuff tail and sew to back of body on Rnds 5-7 (see photo next page).

Basic Dress

Note: A chain 1 at the beginning of a row is for turning your work and does not count as a stitch.

SKIRT

Ch 60.

Rows 1-8: ch 1, turn, dc in each st across (60 sts).

YOKE

Row 9: ch 1, turn, sc2tog across (30 sts).

Row 10: ch 1, turn, *sc in next 3 sts, sc2tog* across (24 sts).

Row 11: ch 1, turn, sc in first 4 sts; for **armhole**, ch 11 loosely, skip next 2 sts; sc in next 12 sts; for **armhole**, ch 11 loosely, skip next 2 sts; sc in last 4 sts (20 sts, 22 ch).

Row 12: ch 1, turn, hdc in each st or ch across (42 sts).

Row 13: ch 1, turn, *sc in next 5 sts, sc2tog* across (36 sts).

Row 14: ch 1, turn, hdc in each st across.

Row 15: ch 1, turn, sc2tog across (18 sts).

Row 16: ch 1, turn, hdc in each st across.

Row 17: for **chain-loop buttonhole**, ch 4 tightly, do not turn; sl st in next 3 sts; for **chain-loop buttonhole**, ch 4 tightly, sl st in next st. Fasten off.

The Basic Dress is fun to make in lots of colors or to embellish with decorative buttons, bows, appliques, etc. The dress is worked flat from the bottom up in rows. If you would like to use buttons larger than 1/4" at the back opening, make bigger buttonholes by making longer chains in Row 17.

SUPPLIES

G6/4mm crochet hook

Small amount of DK, Light Worsted yarn

2 buttons, 1/4"

Sewing thread

EDGE TRIM

Row 18: join with sl st at bottom of skirt, *ch 3, skip 1 st, sl st in next st* across. Fasten off.

FINISHING

Sew 2 buttons to back edge of yoke opposite buttonholes. Sew back edges together leaving top 2" open.

Weave in ends.

Skirt 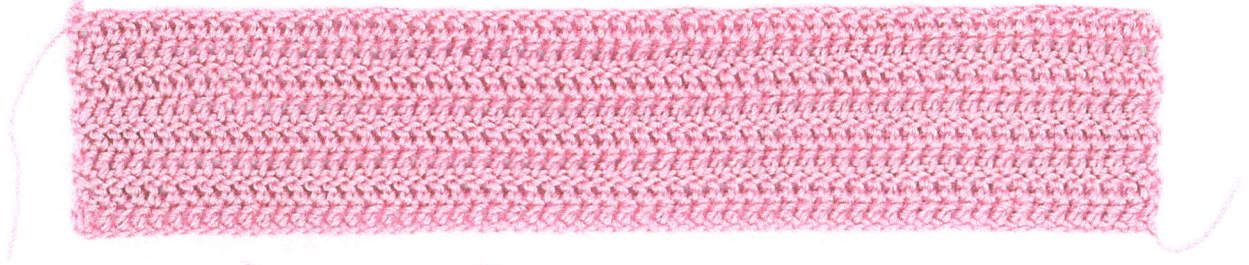 **Rows 1-8**

 Row 9

 Row 11

**Ready to Sew
Back Seam**  Row 18

BASIC DRESS VARIATIONS

With a few simple changes, you can give the Basic Dress an entirely different look.

Watermelon Dress

Ladybug Dress

Work Rows 1–11 and 16–17 in red. Work Rows 12–15 and 18 in black. For dots, pause after Row 8 to embroider French Knots (see page 64) on skirt: For the best results, pierce yarn strands to make French Knots (do not work in the holes between stitches).

Carrot Dress

Work Row 11 with white and omit Row 18. With black, ch 42 tightly, fasten off. Thread tail onto yarn needle and weave through sts at center of yoke. For Watermelon Hat, see page 40.

Work Rows 11–18 in green. Sew buttons to yoke.

Bumblebee Dress

Alternate yellow then black for Rows 1-8. Use yellow for Rows 9-10 and black for Rows 11-18.

For Flower: ch 5 , sl st in 1st st to make a ring. Rnd 1: *ch 6, sl st in ring* 5 times. Fasten off. Tie flower in place with yarn tails. Sew button or bead to center.

Rainbow Dress

Work Rows 1-6 in rainbow colors as shown. Omit Rows 7-8. Work Rows 9-17 in red. Omit Row 18. Sew buttons to yoke.

Pocket Dress

Work Rows 1, 15, 16 & 17 in dark purple. Omit Row 18. For yoke flower, see Bumblebee Dress.

For Pocket, ch 11 loosely. Rows 1-6: ch 1, turn, sc in each st across (11 sts). Fasten off. Sew to dress.

For Ear Flower, see page 41.

Checked Dress

This variation of the Basic Dress features a checked pattern in the skirt section.

Each check is comprised of 3 dc. When changing colors, drop the unused color to the WRONG side. Check your working yarn at the end of each row for tangles and untwist as needed.

SUPPLIES

LIGHT 3

G6/4mm crochet hook

Small amount of DK, Light Worsted yarn in blue and white

4 buttons, 1/4"

Invisible sewing thread

White sewing thread

Note: A chain 1 at the beginning of a row is for turning your work and does not count as a stitch.

SKIRT

With blue, ch 60.

Rows 1-8: ch 1, turn, dc in each st across changing colors between blue and white in last yarn over of every 3rd stitch (60 sts).

Be sure you have ended Row 8 with a blue loop on hook. Cut off white yarn with tail.

YOKE

Row 9: with blue, ch 1, turn, sc2tog across (30 sts).

Row 10: ch 1, turn, *sc in next 3 sts, sc2tog* across (24 sts).

Row 11: ch 1, turn, sc in first 4 sts; for **armhole**, ch 11 loosely, skip next 2 sts; sc in next 12 sts; for **armhole**, ch 11 loosely, skip next 2 sts; sc in last 4 sts (20 sts, 22 ch).

Row 12: ch 1, turn, hdc in each st or ch across (42 sts).

Row 13: ch 1, turn, *sc in next 5 sts, sc2tog* across (36 sts).

Row 14: ch 1, turn, hdc in each st across.

Row 15: ch 1, turn, sc2tog across (18 sts).

Row 16: ch 1, turn, hdc in each st across.

Row 17: for **chain-loop buttonhole**, ch 4 tightly, do not turn; sl st in next 3 sts; for **chain-loop buttonhole**, ch 4 tightly, sl st in next st. Fasten off.

EDGE TRIM

Row 18: join blue with sl st at bottom of skirt, *ch 3, skip 1 st, sl st in next st* across. Fasten off.

FINISHING

Sew 2 buttons to center front of yoke. Sew 2 buttons to back edge of yoke opposite buttonholes. Using invisible thread, sew back edges together leaving top 2" open. Weave in ends.

Skirt 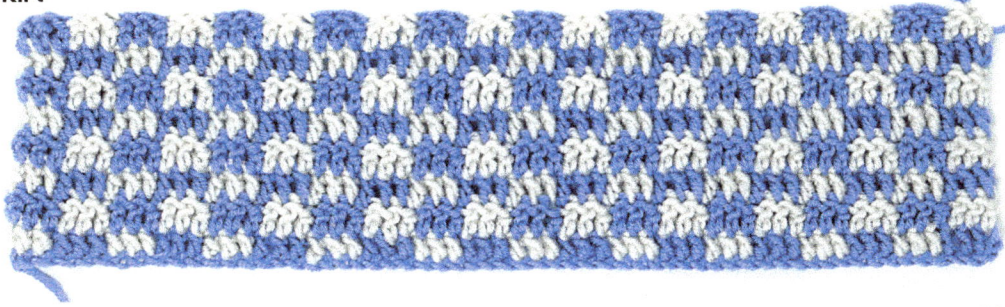 Rows 1-8

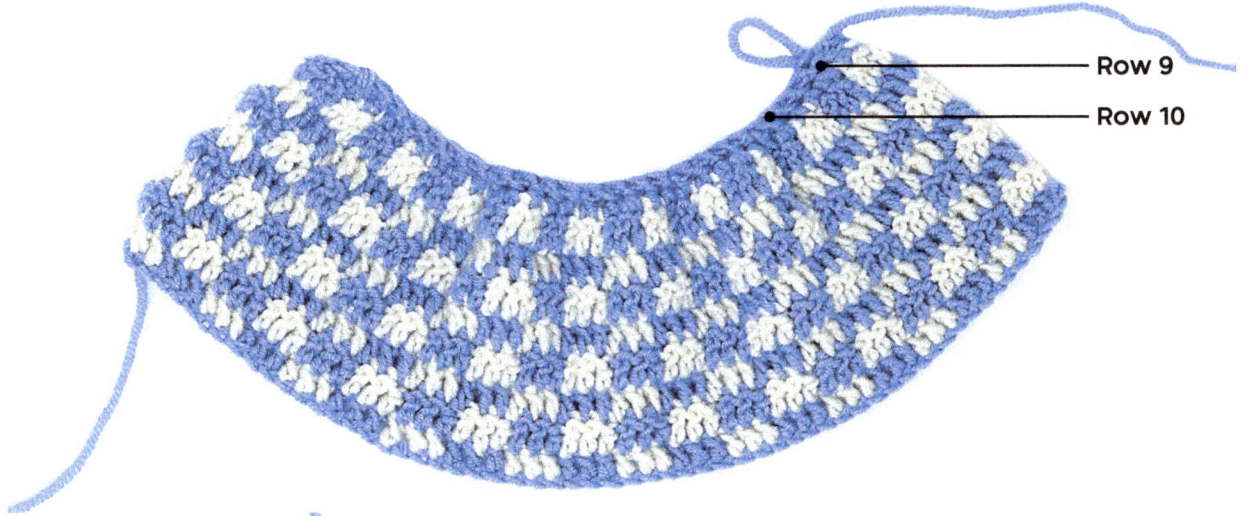 Row 9

Row 10

 Row 11

Ready to Sew Back Seam  Row 18

Overall Dress

SUPPLIES

G6/4mm crochet hook

Small amount of DK, Light Worsted yarn in blue and gold

2 buttons, 3/8"

Sewing thread

The Overall Dress is crocheted with a combination of rounds and rows. First, the skirt is made from the top down; then the bib is added.

Note: A chain 1 at the beginning of a row is for turning your work and does not count as a stitch.

SKIRT

With blue, ch 36, join with sl st to 1st ch to make a ring using care not to twist the chain.

Rnds 1-3: sc in each st around. Place marker for beginning of rnd and move marker up as each rnd is completed.

Rnd 4: *sc in next 5 sts, 2 sc in next st* 6 times (42 sts).

Rnds 5-7: sc in each st around.

Rnd 8: *sc in next 6 sts, 2 sc in next st* 6 times (48 sts).

Rnds 9-16: sc in each st around.

Sl st in next st. Fasten off.

BIB

At upper edge of skirt (Rnd 1), mark the 12 sts at center front to make bib.

Row 1: join blue with sc at right marker, sc in next 11 sts (12 sts).

Row 2: ch 1, turn, sc2tog, sc in next 8 sts, sc2tog (10 sts).

Row 3: ch 1, turn, sc in each st across.

Row 4: ch 1, turn, sc2tog, sc in next 6 sts, sc2tog (8 sts). Fasten off.

POCKET

With blue, ch 11.

Rows 1-6: ch 1, turn, sc in each st across (11 sts). Fasten off. Weave in ends.

STRAPS (MAKE 2)

With blue, ch 21; for **buttonhole**, skip first 4 chs from hook; sc in last 17 chs. Fasten off.

FINISHING

For decorative topstitching around hemline, waistline, bib and pocket, turn dress so that wrong side faces you. Insert hook in st at edge, pull up a loop of gold, and sl st in each st around. Pull tails to wrong side and weave in ends. Sew buttons to corners of bib and attach straps with buttonholes. Sew back of straps to back of dress spaced 1 1/2" apart crossing straps as shown in photo. Sew straps together at the X where they cross. Sew pocket in place with sewing thread.

Basic Shirt

Make 2

SUPPLIES

G6/4mm crochet hook

Small amount of DK, Light Worsted yarn

LIGHT 3

Two identical pieces are crocheted flat in rows and sewn together to make this easy top.

Note: A chain 1 at the beginning of a row is for turning your work and does not count as a stitch.

SHIRT (MAKE 2)

Ch 18.

Rows 1-4: ch 1, turn, dc in each st across (18 sts).

Rows 5-7: ch 1, turn, dc in next 15 sts (15 sts).

Row 8: ch 4, turn, dc in 2nd ch from hook and each remaining ch or st across (18 sts).

FINISHING

Stack pieces and sew together across shoulders. Sew up sides leaving 1" open to make armholes. Weave in ends.

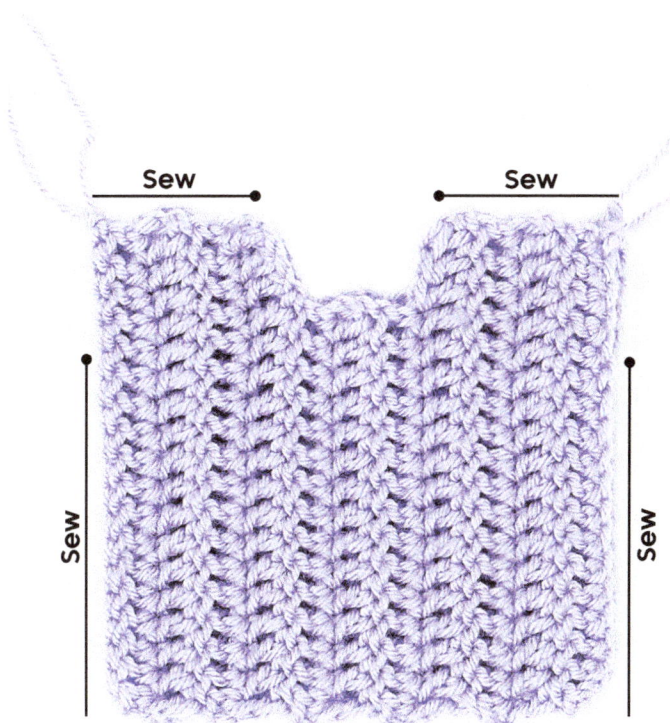

Sew   Sew

Sew   Sew

BASIC SHIRT VARIATIONS

Transform the Basic Shirt with appliques, a collar, buttons and crocheted checks.

Carrot Applique

Flower Applique

Make flower following Ear Flower instructions on page 41. Sew button at center.

Collar Shirt

Make collar following instructions on page 24. Sew buttons to center front.

SUPPLIES

G6/4mm crochet hook

Small amount of DK, Light Worsted yarn in orange and green

The carrot is worked entirely in a magic ring. When the ring is pulled tight, the carrot appears like magic!

CARROT

With orange, make a magic ring, ch 1. All stitches are worked into the magic ring unless otherwise instructed.

Rnd 1: 2 tr, 1 dc, 4 sc, 1 dc, 1 tr, 1 dc, 4 sc, 1 dc—working all prior sts in ring; join to next st with sl st. Pull ring closed tight. Fasten off. Weave in ends. Pinch carrot into shape.

CARROT TOP

Join green with sl st at center top of carrot, ch 4.

Row 1: sl st in 2nd ch from hook and in each remaining ch across, sl st into orange starting point (4 sts).

Rows 2-3: ch 4, sl st in 2nd ch from hook and in each remaining ch across, sl st into orange starting point (4 sts). Fasten off. Weave in ends.

22

Checked Shirt

SUPPLIES

G6/4mm crochet hook

Small amount of DK, Light Worsted yarn in turquoise and pink

3 buttons, 1/4"

Invisible sewing thread

White sewing thread

Two identical pieces are crocheted in rows and sewn together to make this shirt.

Each check comprised of 3 dc: When changing colors, drop the unused color to the WRONG side; check your working yarn at the end of each row for tangles and untwist as needed.

Note: A chain 1 at the beginning of a row is for turning your work and does not count as a stitch.

SHIRT (MAKE 2)

With turquoise, ch 18.

Rows 1-4: ch 1, turn, dc in each st across changing colors between turquoise and pink in last yarn over of every 3rd stitch (18 sts).

Rows 5-7: ch 1, turn, dc in next 15 sts changing colors between turquoise and pink in last yarn over of every 3rd stitch; **do not change color in last st of Row 7** (15 sts).

Row 8: ch 4, turn, dc in 2nd ch from hook and each remaining ch or st across changing colors between turquoise and pink in last yarn over of every 3rd stitch (18 sts).

Rows 9-11: ch 1, turn, dc in each st across changing colors between turquoise and pink in last yarn over of every 3rd stitch (18 sts).

Row 12: ch 1, turn, sc in each across. Fasten off.

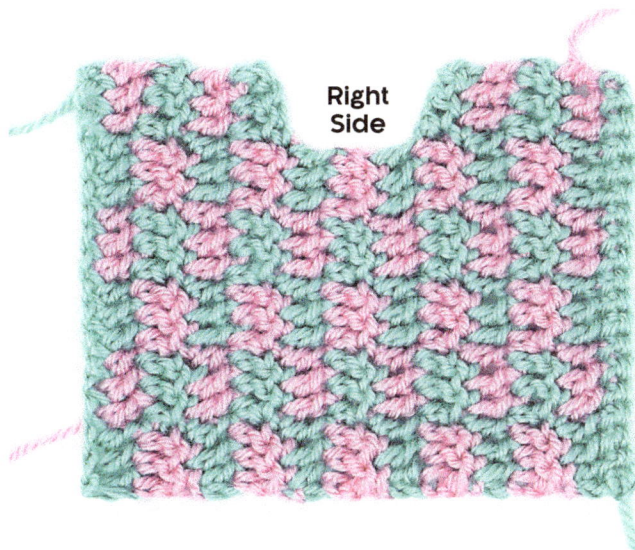

Right Side

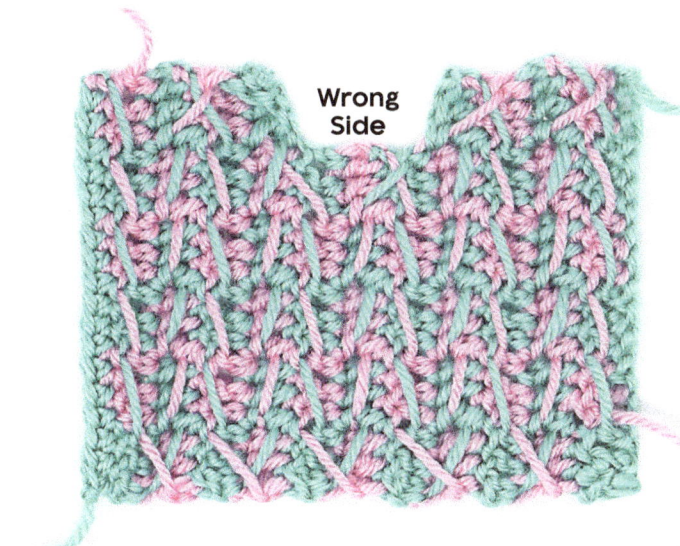

Wrong Side

23

Stack pieces and sew together across shoulders. Sew up sides leaving 1" open to make armholes.

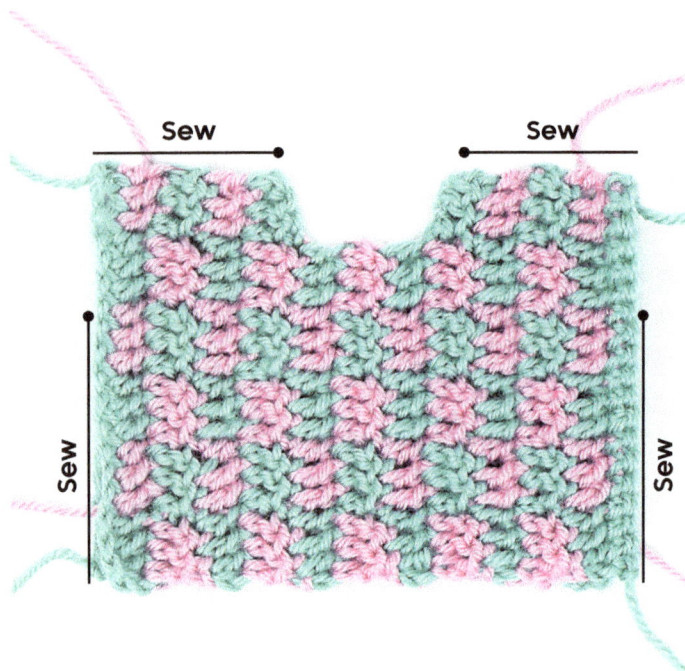

COLLAR

Mark center front and center back of neckline.

FIRST SIDE

Join turquoise with sl st at center back.

Row 1: ch 1, sc around neck edge until you reach center front (approx. 15 sts).

Rows 2-4: ch 1, turn, sc in each st across. Fasten off.

SECOND SIDE

Join turquoise with sl st at center front.

Row 1: ch 1, sc around neck edge until you reach center back (approx. 15 sts).

Rows 2-4: ch 1, turn, sc in each st across. Fasten off.

FINISHING

Weave in ends. Sew buttons to center front.

PANTS & SHORTS
Jeans

Rnds 14-17: sc in each st around.

Rnd 18: to make **tail slit**, sc in each st around until nearing end of round (this is back of pants), then pause to mark the 6 sts at center back. Continue sc to first marker, ch 6, skip 6 sts.

Rnd 19: after 6 skipped sts, sc in each st or ch around to center back.

Rnds 20-22: sc in each st around (36 sts).

Sl st in next st. Fasten off. Weave in ends.

FINISHING

Sew the opening at crotch closed. For decorative topstitching around pant legs and waistline, turn pants so that wrong side faces you. Insert hook in st at edge, pull up a loop of gold, and sl st in each st around. Pull tails to wrong side and weave in ends. Thread a yarn needle with elastic cord and weave through back of stitches around waist edge. Try jeans on bunny to get the right tension so it's not too loose or too tight. Tie a knot to secure elastic and weave in ends.

SUPPLIES

LIGHT 3

G6/4mm crochet hook

Small amount of DK, Light Worsted yarn in blue and gold

Stretch Magic clear elastic bead cord (.7mm)

The jeans are crocheted in rounds, starting with the legs. A slit is made at the back for the bunny's tail. Clear elastic beading cord makes terrific waistband elastic.

FIRST LEG

With blue, ch 18, join with sl st to 1st ch to make a ring using care not to twist the chain.

Rnds 1-12: sc in each st around. Place marker for beginning of rnd and move marker up as each rnd is completed. Fasten off.

SECOND LEG

Repeat first leg but do not fasten off.

Rnd 13: join first leg by working around the 18 sts of first leg and then the 18 sts of second leg (36 sts).

Pants

Work same as Jeans but omit the decorative topstitching.

Shorts

SUPPLIES

G6/4mm crochet hook

Small amount of DK, Light Worsted yarn

Stretch Magic clear elastic bead cord (.7mm)

The shorts are crocheted in rounds, starting with the legs. A slit is made at the back for the bunny's tail.

FIRST LEG

Ch 18, join with sl st to 1st ch to make a ring using care not to twist the chain.

Rnds 1-5: sc in each st around. Place marker for beginning of rnd and move marker up as each rnd is completed. Fasten off.

SECOND LEG

Repeat first leg but do not fasten off.

Rnd 6: Join first leg by working around the 18 sts of first leg and then the 18 sts of second leg (36 sts).

Rnds 7-10: sc in each st around.

Rnd 11: to make **tail slit**, sc in each st around until nearing end of round (this is back of shorts), then pause to mark the 6 sts at center back. Continue sc to first marker, ch 6, skip 6 sts.

Rnd 12: after 6 skipped sts, sc in each st or ch around to center back.

Rnds 13-15: sc in each st around (36 sts).

Sl st in next st. Fasten off.

FINISHING

Sew the opening at crotch closed. Weave in ends. Thread a yarn needle with elastic cord and weave through back of stitches around waist edge. Try shorts on bunny to get the right tension so it's not too loose or too tight. Tie a knot to secure elastic and weave in ends.

Gardening Shorts

Jeans Shorts

Work same as Shorts, adding a pocket to each side. For Pockets, ch 6 loosely. Rows 1-6: ch 1, turn, sc in each st across (6 sts). Fasten off. Sew to sides.

Work same as Shorts adding decorative topstitching around pant legs and waistline before elastic is inserted. To topstitch, turn so that wrong side faces you. Insert hook in st at edge, pull up a loop of gold, and sl st in each st around. Pull tails to wrong side and weave in ends.

Overalls

SUPPLIES

G6/4mm crochet hook

Small amount of DK, Light Worsted yarn in blue and gold

2 buttons, 3/8"

Sewing thread

The overalls are crocheted with a combination of rounds and rows, starting with the legs. A slit is made at the back for the bunny's tail.

Note: A chain 1 at the beginning of a row is for turning your work and does not count as a stitch.

FIRST LEG

With blue, ch 18, join with sl st to 1st ch to make a ring using care not to twist the chain.

Rnds 1-12: sc in each st around. Place marker for beginning of rnd and move marker up as each rnd is completed (18 sts). Fasten off.

SECOND LEG

Repeat first leg but do not fasten off.

Rnd 13: Join first leg by working around the 18 sts of first leg and then the 18 sts of second leg (36 sts).

Rnds 14-17: sc in each st around.

Rnd 18: to make **tail slit**, sc in each st around until nearing end of round (this is back of overalls), then pause to mark the 6 sts at center back. Continue sc to first marker, ch 6, skip 6 sts.

Rnd 19: after 6 skipped sts, sc in each st or ch around to center back.

Rnds 20-22: sc in each st around (36 sts).

Sl st in next st. Fasten off.

BIB

Mark 18 sts at center front of pants section to make bib.

Row 1: join blue with sc at right marker, sc in next 17 sts (18 sts).

Row 2: ch 1, turn, sc2tog, sc in next 14 sts, sc2tog (16 sts).

Row 3: ch 1, turn, sc2tog, sc in next 12 sts, sc2tog (14 sts).

Row 4: ch 1, turn, sc in each st across.

Row 5: ch 1, turn, sc2tog, sc in next 10 sts, sc2tog (12 sts).

Row 6: ch 1, turn, sc in each st across.

Row 7: ch 1, turn, sc2tog, sc in next 8 sts, sc2tog (10 sts).

Row 8: ch 1, turn, sc in each st across.

Row 9: ch 1, turn, sc2tog, sc in next 6 sts, sc2tog (8 sts). Fasten off. Weave in ends.

POCKET

With blue, ch 11.

Rows 1-6: ch 1, turn, sc in each st across (11 sts). Fasten off. Weave in ends.

STRAPS (MAKE 2)

With blue, chain 23; for **buttonhole**, skip first 4 chs from hook; sc in last 19 chs. Fasten off.

FINISHING

Sew opening at crotch closed. For decorative topstitching around pant legs, waistline, bib and pocket, turn so that wrong side of overalls faces you. Insert hook in st at edge, pull up a loop of gold, and sl st in each st around. Pull tails to wrong side and weave in ends.

Sew buttons to corners of bib and attach straps with buttonholes. Sew back of straps to back of overalls spaced 1 1/2" apart crossing straps as shown in photo. Sew straps together at the X where they cross. Sew pocket to front with sewing thread.

COSTUMES

The Garden Fairy works her magic on the garden using her sprinkling can while Captain Compost, the garden superhero, uses the power of compost and his shovel. (See Garden Accessories, pages 52-54.)

Garden Fairy

SUPPLIES

G6/4mm crochet hook

Small amount of DK, Light Worsted yarn in medium green and light green

1 button, 1/2"

2 sew-on snap fasteners

Sewing thread

The tutu is worked flat from the top down, back and forth in rows, then sewn up at the back. The panty is worked separately and sewn in place.

Note: A chain 1 at the beginning of a row is for turning your work and does not count as a stitch.

BODICE

With medium green, chain 25.

Row 1: sc in second ch from hook and in each remaining ch across (24 sts).

Row 2: ch 1, turn,*sc in next 3 sts, 2 sc in next st* across (30 sts).

Row 3: ch 1, turn,*sc in next 4 sts, 2 sc in next st* across (36 sts).

Rows 4-8: ch 1, turn, sc in each st across.

SKIRT

Row 9: ch 1, turn, 2 hdc in each st across working in **back loops only** (72 sts).

Row 10: resuming work in both loops, ch 1, turn, 2 hdc in each st across (144 sts).

Row 11: ch 1, turn, hdc in each st across changing to light green in last st.

Row 12: ch 1, turn, sc in each st across. Fasten off.

Sew up back from edge of ruffle through Row 5.

PANTY

With medium green, make underwear (see page 38) omitting the elastic. Nest underwear inside bodice, wrong sides together, so that center backs meet. Sew waist of underwear to unworked loops of Row 9. Turn right side out.

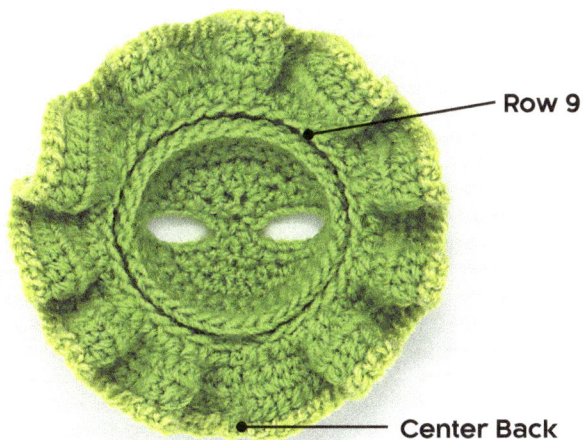

Row 9

Center Back

STRAPS (MAKE 2)

With medium green, chain 11; sc in second ch from hook and in each remaining ch across (10 sts). Fasten off.

Place tutu on bunny to mark position for straps so that straps align with bunny's shoulders. Use yarn tails to sew straps in place, right side up, to bodice front. Sew one half of snap fasteners to back of straps (right side) and the other halves to back of bodice (wrong side).

FINISHING

For **chain-loop buttonhole**, join with sl st at left side of bodice, ch 5 tightly, sl st in next st, fasten off. Sew button on opposite edge of bodice. Weave in yarn ends.

EAR FLOWER

Make a green Ear Flower following instructions on page 41.

SHOES

Make green Shoes following pattern on page 36.

Captain Compost

SUPPLIES

G6/4mm crochet hook

Small amount of DK, Light Worsted yarn in brown, green and yellow

1 button, 3/8"

2 hook and eye fasteners

2 sew-on snap fasteners

Sewing thread

LIGHT 3

Row 30: ch 1, turn, *sc in next 9 sts, sc2tog* across (30 sts).

Row 31: ch 1, turn, *sc in next 3 sts, sc2tog* across (24 sts).

Row 32: ch 1, turn, *sc in next 6 sts, sc2tog* across (21 sts).

Row 33: ch 1, turn, *sc in next 5 sts, sc2tog* across (18 sts).

Row 34: ch 1, turn, sc in first 2 sts; for **armhole**, ch 10 loosely, skip next 2 sts; sc in next 10 sts; for **armhole**, ch 10 loosely, skip next 2 sts; sc in last 2 sts. This creates 2 chain arches where you will work the sleeves (14 sts, 20 ch).

Fasten off.

SLEEVES (MAKE 2)

Join brown with sc at underarm and work in rnds. The 1st rnd is worked into the 2 skipped sts of Row 34 and the chain arch.

Rnds 1-13: sc in each st around (12 sts).

Sl st in next st. Fasten off.

FINISHING

Join brown with sl st at left corner of neckline.

Rnd 1: *dc in next 2 sts, dc2tog* around neck edge; ch 1, do not turn, sc in each st around back opening. Fasten off.

Sew the opening at crotch closed. Weave in ends.

Sew button on one side at top of back opening. Use space between dc for buttonhole. Sew hooks on one side of back opening and eyes on the other side.

The jumpsuit is crocheted with a combination of rounds and rows, starting with the legs. A slit is made at the back of the jumpsuit for the bunny's tail.

Note: A chain 1 at the beginning of a row is for turning your work and does not count as a stitch.

JUMPSUIT

FIRST LEG

With brown, ch 18, join with sl st to 1st ch to make a ring using care not to twist the chain.

Rnds 1-12: sc in each st around. Place marker for beginning of rnd and move marker up as each rnd is completed (18 sts). Fasten off.

SECOND LEG, SHORTS & BELT SECTIONS

Repeat first leg; change to green in last st, do not fasten off.

Rnd 13: Join first leg by working around the 18 sts of first leg and then the 18 sts of second leg (36 sts).

Rnds 14-17: sc in each st around.

Rnd 18: to make **tail slit**, sc in each st around until nearing end of round (this is back of jumpsuit), then pause to mark the 6 sts at center back. Continue sc to first marker, ch 6, skip 6 sts.

Rnd 19: after 6 skipped sts, sc in each st around to center back.

Rnd 20: sc in each st around; change to yellow in last st (36 sts).

Rnds 21-22: sc in each st around; change to brown in last st.

SHIRT SECTION

Change to working in rows to make back opening.

Rows 23-28: ch 1, turn, sc in each st across (36 sts).

Row 29: ch 1, turn, *sc in next 10 sts, sc2tog* across (33 sts).

TRIANGLE

With yellow, ch 6.

Rows 1-5: ch 1, turn, sc in 3rd st from hook and each remaining st across.

Rnd 6: ch 1, sc around perimeter making 3 sts in same st at corners. Fasten off. Weave in ends. Sew to chest of jumpsuit.

LETTER

With green, ch 9 tightly. Fasten off.

Shape chain into letter "C" to fit center of triangle and pull tails through to wrong side. Sew in place on center of triangle with sewing needle and thread. Tie tails together. Weave in ends.

CAPE

With green, ch 12.

Row 1: ch 1, turn, dc in each st across (12 sts).

Row 2: ch 1, turn, *dc in next st, 2 dc in next st* across (18 sts).

Rows 3-8: ch 1, turn, 2 dc in first st, dc across until last st, 2 dc in last st (30 sts at Row 8).

Rows 9-15: ch 1, turn, dc in each st across.

Rnd 16: for **edge trim**, ch 1 and work forward to sc in each st along first side, top and second side making 3 sts in same st at corners.

Fasten off. Weave in ends.

Sew one half of snap fasteners to wrong side of cape at upper corners; sew other halves to right side of jumpsuit at top of shoulders.

MASK

Note: When you are instructed to crochet into a chain space, just insert your hook into the space underneath the chain to make your stitch. For a video demo, visit my Pinterest board of Amigurumi Tutorials (see page 65).

With green, ch 36, join with sl st to 1st ch to make a ring using care not to twist the chain.

Rnds 1-2: sc in each st around. Place marker for beginning of rnd and move marker up as each rnd is completed (36 sts).

Rnd 3: sc in next 11 sts; for **eyehole**, ch 8, skip 6 sts; for **nose bridge**, sc in next 2 sts; for **eyehole**, ch 8, skip 6 sts; sc in next 11 sts (24 sts, 16 ch).

Rnd 4: sc in next 11 sts, 10 dc into chain space, sc in next 2 sts, 10 dc into chain space, sc in next 11 sts (44 sts).

Sl st in next st. Fasten off. Weave in ends.

BOOTS

Make green Boots following pattern on page 37.

OUTERWEAR
Cardigan

SUPPLIES

G6/4mm crochet hook

Small amount of DK, Light Worsted yarn

1 button, 1/2"

Sewing thread

The cardigan is worked flat in 2 pieces. The fit is sized to be worn over other garments.

Note: A chain 1 at the beginning of a row is for turning your work and does not count as a stitch.

SIDE (MAKE 2)

Ch 40.

Rows 1–8: ch 1, turn, dc in next 10 sts, sc in next 20 sts, dc in next 10 sts (40 sts). Fasten off.

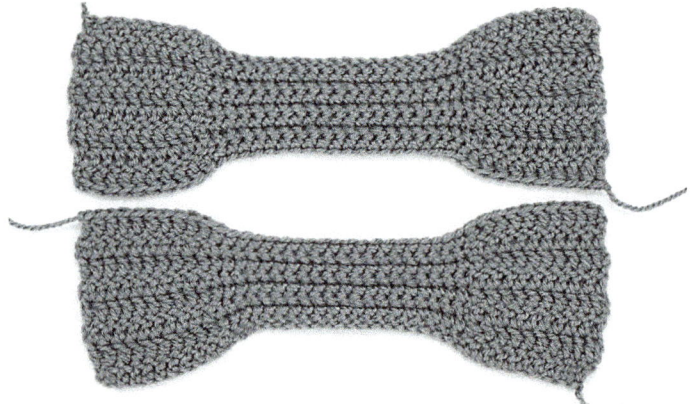

Stack sides with wrong sides facing and sew 15 sts together (about 3") to make center back seam. (See A.)

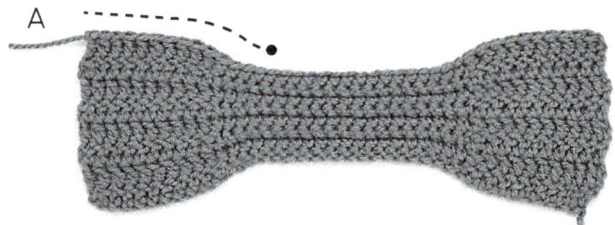

Fold pieces in half crosswise and sew 10 sts together (about 2") to connect sides. (See B.)

SLEEVES (MAKE 2)

Join with sc at underarm.

Rnds 1–3: sc in each st around. Place marker for beginning of rnd and move marker up as each rnd is completed.

Sl st in next st. Fasten off.

FINISHING

Sew button to one front edge at point where sc meets dc. For **buttonhole**, join with sl st to edge opposite button and make a chain long enough to go around button. Sl st in next st. Fasten off. Weave in ends.

Jacket

The jacket is worked flat in rows. The fit is sized to be worn over other garments.

SUPPLIES

LIGHT 3

G6/4mm crochet hook

Small amount of DK, Light Worsted yarn in purple and gray

4 hook and eye fasteners

Sewing thread

Note: A chain 1 at the beginning of a row is for turning your work and does not count as a stitch.

FRONT (MAKE 2)

With purple, ch 18.

Rows 1-6: ch 1, turn, sc in each st across (18 sts).

Rows 7-11: ch 1, turn, sc in next 14 sts (14 sts). Fasten off.

BACK

With purple, ch 18.

Rows 1-6: ch 1, turn, sc in each st across (18 sts).

Rows 7-15: ch 1, turn, sc in next 14 sts (14 sts).

Row 16: ch 5, turn, sc in 2nd ch from hook and each remaining ch or st across (18 sts).

Rows 17-21: ch 1, turn, sc in each st across (18 sts).

Fasten off.

SLEEVES (MAKE 2)

With purple, ch 5.

Rows 1-18: ch 1, turn, sc in each st across (5 sts).

Row 19: ch 3, do not turn, dc across ends of rows on next long side (18 sts). Fasten off.

FINISHING

Sew front pieces to back at shoulders. Align center of sleeve with shoulder seam and sew in place. (See photo below.) Fold piece in half crosswise so that hem edges of fronts and back meet. Sew together along underarm and side.

With right side facing you, join purple with sl st at **neck edge**: ch 2, *dc in next 3 sts, dc2tog* around. Fasten off.

With right side facing you, join purple with sl st at **lower edge**: ch 2, dc in each st around. Fasten off.

For **mock zipper**, join gray with sc to front edges and sc in each st across. Fasten off. Weave in ends.

Sew the hooks onto one side and the eyes on the other side of the front opening.

FOOTWEAR

Shoes

SUPPLIES

G6/4mm crochet hook

Small amount of DK, Light Worsted yarn

Make a magic ring, ch 1.

Rnd 1: 6 sc in ring, pull ring closed tight (6 sts).

Rnd 2: 2 sc in each st around. Place marker for beginning of rnd and move marker up as each rnd is completed (12 sts).

Rnd 3: *sc in next st, 2 sc in next st* 6 times (18 sts).

Rnd 4: *sc in next 2 sts, 2 sc in next st* 6 times (24 sts).

Rnd 5: sc in each st around.

Rnd 6: *sc in next 2 sts, sc2tog* 6 times (18 sts).

Rnd 7: sc in next 6 sts, sc2tog 3 times, sc in next 6 sts (15 sts).

Rnd 8: sl st in each st around. Fasten off. Weave in end.

Make a 2nd identical shoe.

Sneakers

SUPPLIES

G6/4mm crochet hook

Small amount of DK, Light Worsted yarn in plum and gold

With gold, make a magic ring, ch 1.

Rnd 1: 6 sc in ring, pull ring closed tight (6 sts).

Rnd 2: 2 sc in each st around. Place marker for beginning of rnd and move marker up as each rnd is completed (12 sts).

Rnd 3: *sc in next st, 2 sc in next st* 6 times (18 sts).

Rnd 4: *sc in next 2 sts, 2 sc in next st* 6 times (24 sts).

Rnd 5: sc in each st around; change to plum in last st.

Rnd 6: *sc in next 2 sts, sc2tog* 6 times (18 sts).

Weave in loose tails now before shoe top gets too narrow.

Rnd 7: sc in next 6 sts, sc2tog 3 times, sc in next 6 sts (15 sts).

Rnd 8: sc in each st around.

Rnd 9: sl st in each st around. Fasten off. Weave in end.

Embroider laces as shown in photos and tie ends in a bow. Note: To keep laces from fraying, dip tips in clear-drying white glue. Make a 2nd identical shoe.

Boots

SUPPLIES

G6/4mm crochet hook

Small amount of DK, Light Worsted yarn

LIGHT 3

Make a magic ring, ch 1.

Rnd 1: 6 sc in ring, pull ring closed tight (6 sts).

Rnd 2: 2 sc in each st around. Place marker for beginning of rnd and move marker up as each rnd is completed (12 sts).

Rnd 3: *sc in next st, 2 sc in next st* 6 times (18 sts).

Rnd 4: *sc in next 2 sts, 2 sc in next st* 6 times (24 sts).

Rnd 5: sc in each st around.

Rnd 6: *sc in next 2 sts, sc2tog* 6 times (18 sts).

Weave in starting tail now before boot gets too narrow.

Rnd 7: sc in next 6 sts, sc2tog 3 times, sc in next 6 sts (15 sts).

Rnds 8-13: sc in each st around.

Sl st in next st. Fasten off. Weave in end.

Make a 2nd identical shoe.

For a cute variation, use a contrasting color for Rnd 13.

Work Boots

SUPPLIES

G6/4mm crochet hook

Small amount of DK, Light Worsted yarn in off-white, caramel and brown

LIGHT 3

With off-white, make a magic ring, ch 1.

Rnd 1: 6 sc in ring, pull ring closed tight (6 sts).

Rnd 2: 2 sc in each st around. Place marker for beginning of rnd and move marker up as each rnd is completed (12 sts).

Rnd 3: *sc in next st, 2 sc in next st* 6 times (18 sts).

Rnd 4: *sc in next 2 sts, 2 sc in next st* 6 times; change to caramel in last st (24 sts).

Rnd 5: working in **back loops only**, sc in each st around.

Rnd 6: resuming work in both loops, *sc in next 2 sts, sc2tog* 6 times (18 sts).

Weave in loose tails now before boot gets too narrow.

Rnd 7: sc in next 6 sts, sc2tog 3 times, sc in next 6 sts (15 sts).

Rnds 8-11: sc in each st around. Sl st in next st. Fasten off.

FINISHING

With sole facing up, join brown with sl st in an unworked front loop of Rnd 5 and sl st in each front loop around. Weave in ends. Embroider laces as shown in photos. Tie ends in a bow. Note: To keep laces from fraying, dip tips in clear-drying white glue. Make a 2nd identical shoe.

ACCESSORIES

Underwear

SUPPLIES

G6/4mm crochet hook

Small amount of DK, Light Worsted yarn

Stretch Magic clear elastic bead cord (.7mm)

The underwear is worked flat, back and forth in rows.

Note: A chain 1 at the beginning of a row is for turning your work and does not count as a stitch.

Ch 19.

Row 1: sc in 2nd ch from hook and in each remaining ch across (18 sts).

Row 2: ch 1, turn, sc in each st across (18 sts).

Row 3: ch 1, turn, sc2tog, sc in next 14 sts, sc2tog (16 sts).

Row 4: ch 1, turn, sc2tog, sc in next 12 sts, sc2tog (14 sts).

Row 5: ch 1, turn, sc2tog, sc in next 10 sts, sc2tog (12 sts).

Row 6: ch 1, turn, sc2tog twice, sc in next 4 sts, sc2tog twice (8 sts).

Row 7: ch 1, turn, sc2tog across (4 sts).

Row 8: ch 1, turn, sc2tog twice (2 sts).

Row 9: ch 1, turn, sc2tog (1 st).

Row 10: ch 1, turn, 2 sc in next st (2 sts).

Row 11: ch 1, turn, 2 sc in next 2 sts (4 sts).

Row 12: ch 1, turn, 2 sc in next 4 sts (8 sts).

Row 13: ch 1, turn, 2 sc in next 2 sts, sc in next 4 sts, 2 sc in next 2 sts (12 sts).

Row 14: ch 1, turn, 2 sc in next st, sc in next 10 sts, 2 sc in next st (14 sts).

Row 15: ch 1, turn, 2 sc in next st, sc in next 12 sts, 2 sc in next st (16 sts).

Row 16: ch 1, turn, 2 sc in next st, sc in next 4 sts; for **tail opening**, ch 6 loosely, skip next 6 sts; sc in next 4 sts, 2 sc in next st (12 sts and 6 ch).

Row 17: ch 1, turn, sc in each st or ch across (18 sts).

Row 18: ch 1, turn, sc in each st across. Fasten off.

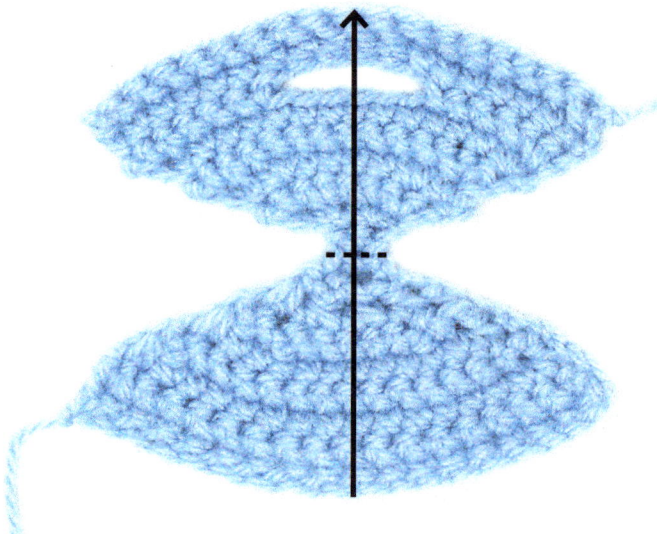

FINISHING

Fold underwear in half crosswise and sew together at sides from waist down 1/2". Work a round of sc around leg openings, joining the new yarn with sl st and ending with sl st. Weave in yarn ends. Thread a yarn needle with elastic cord and weave through back of stitches around waist edge. Try underwear on bunny to get the right tension so it's not too loose or too tight. Tie a knot to secure elastic and weave in ends.

Gardening Apron

SUPPLIES

G6/4mm crochet hook

Small amount of DK, Light Worsted yarn in orange, green & brown

Sewing thread in brown

LIGHT 3

Note: A chain 1 at the beginning of a row is for turning your work and does not count as a stitch.

APRON

With orange, ch 8.

Row 1: ch 1, turn, sc in each st across (8 sts).

Rows 2-10: ch 1, turn, 2 sc in 1st st, sc in each st across until 1 st remains, 2 sc in last st (26 sts at end of Row 10).

Rows 11-20: ch 1, turn, sc in each st across.

Fasten off. Weave in ends.

POCKET

With green, ch 14.

Rows 1-6: ch 1, turn, sc in each st across; change to brown in last st (14 sts).

Row 7: ch 1, do not turn, sc in each st around next 3 sides making 3 sts in same st at corners. Fasten off. Weave in ends.

FINISHING

For **first tie**, ch 50 with brown; join with sc to armhole edge and sc in each st across armhole edge; to finish tie, ch 50. Fasten off. Repeat on other side for **second tie**. Weave in ends. Sew pocket to front of apron with thread.

Scarf

SUPPLIES

G6/4mm crochet hook

Small amount of DK, Light Worsted yarn in green and peach

LIGHT 3

Note: A chain 1 at the beginning of a row is for turning your work and does not count as a stitch.

Each stripe is comprised of 2 rows.

With peach, ch 4.

Rows 1-70: ch 1, turn, sc in each st across changing to alternate color in last st of every other row (4 sts).

Note: Pull yarn gently to tighten after each color change. Work over unused yarn by holding it against row.

Fasten off. Weave in ends.

FINISHING

To make **fringe**, cut four 3-inch strands of yarn from each color. Put hook through first stitch on one end of scarf. Catch strand in the middle and pull part way through stitch. Place the 2 tail ends over hook and pull them all the way through loop on hook. Pull tails tight. Continue making fringe across both ends of scarf by alternating the colors. Separate yarn plies and trim ends even.

Gardening Hat

Rnds 2-3: dc in each st around.

Rnd 4: working in **front loops only**, 2 dc in each st around (60 sts).

Rnd 5: resuming work in both loops, dc in each st around; change to brown in last st.

Rnd 6: sc in each st around.

Sl st in next st. Fasten off. Weave in ends.

CORD TIES

With brown, make a 16" chain. Weave chain through sts of Rnd 3 around front half of hat. Be sure ties hang down inside hat. Using yarn needle, pull ends through wooden bead and knot each tip. Trim ends.

Watermelon Hat

The Gardening Hat is Honey Bunny's favorite everyday hat. It's easy to change it in lots of ways using different colors and embellishments. The Watermelon Hat and Sun Hat are two variations.

SUPPLIES

G6/4mm crochet hook

Small amount of DK, Light Worsted yarn in gold and brown

1 wooden bead

The gardening hat is worked in rounds from the top down. The open top accommodates Honey Bunny's ears.

HAT

Ch 24, join with sl st to 1st ch to make a ring using care not to twist the chain.

Rnd 1: *dc in next 3 sts, 2 dc in next st* 6 times. Place marker for beginning of rnd and move marker up as each rnd is completed (30 sts).

Follow instructions for Gardening Hat using peach for Rnds 1-4, white for Rnd 5 and green for Rnd 6. Use black for Cord Ties.

Sun Hat

Follow instructions for Gardening Hat using pink for Rnds 1-6 and turquoise for Rnd 6. Omit Cord Ties. Make the flower following Ear Flower instructions and sew a button at the center.

Beanie

SUPPLIES

G6/4mm crochet hook

Small amount of DK, Light Worsted yarn

The beanie is worked from the top down in rounds. A hole at the top accommodates Honey Bunny's ears.

Ch 24, join with sl st to 1st ch to make a ring using care not to twist the chain.

Rnd 1: *sc in next 3 sts, 2 sc in next st* 6 times. Place marker for beginning of rnd and move marker up as each rnd is completed (30 sts).

Rnd 2: *sc in next 4 sts, 2 sc in next st* 6 times (36 sts).

Rnd 3: *sc in next 5 sts, 2 sc in next st* 6 times (42 sts).

Rnds 4-?: sc in each st around until beanie reaches top of bunny's eyes, about 10 rnds. Sl st in next st. Fasten off. Weave in ends.

Ear Flower

SUPPLIES

G6/4mm crochet hook

Small amount of DK, Light Worsted yarn

Make a magic ring, ch 1. All sts except the chs are worked into the ring.

Rnd 1: *3 dc, sl st, ch 1* 5 times.

Fasten off. Pull ring closed tight and knot tails together.

For ear loop, join with sl st at one side of flower and make a chain long enough to fit around bunny's ear. Fasten off. Sew tail to opposite side of flower. Weave in ends.

Backpack

SUPPLIES

G6/4mm crochet hook

Small amount of DK, Light Worsted yarn in gray and blue

Stretch Magic clear elastic bead cord (.7mm)

1 button, 3/8"

1 sew-on snap fastener

Sewing thread

The backpack is crocheted with a combination of rows and rounds, starting with a rectangle for the bottom, then working around it to create the sides.

BOTTOM

With gray, ch 12.

Rows 1-6: ch 1, turn sc in each st across (12 sts).

SIDES

Continue working forward in rounds.

Rnd 1: do not turn, sc in each st around rectangle making 6 sts across each short side and 12 sts across each long side (36 sts).

Rnd 2: working in **back loops only**, sc in each st around.

Rnds 3-13: resuming work in both loops, sc in each st around. Flatten backpack and mark the 12 sts across center back of bag. This is where the flap will be made.

Rnd 14: sc in each st around until you reach marker for left side of flap.

FLAP

Now work in rows.

Rows 1-6: ch 1, turn, sc in next 12 sts (12 sts).

Rows 7-10: ch 1, turn, sc2tog, sc in each st across until 2 sts remain, sc2tog (4 sts at end of Row 10).

Fasten off. Weave in end.

STRAP

With gray, ch 50.

Row 1: ch 1, turn, sc in each st across (50 sts).

Fasten off.

POCKET (MAKE 2)

With gray, ch 6.

Rows 1-6: ch 1, turn, sc in each st across; change to blue in last st (6 sts).

Row 7: sl st in each st across.

Fasten off. Weave in ends.

FINISHING

Join blue with sl st at base of flap and sl st in each st around flap and open edge of bag. Fasten off. Thread yarn needle with elastic cord, attach at base of flap, and weave through back of stitches around open edge of bag, going along the sides and front only. (Do not weave elastic along back side of bag.) Knot securely. Sew pockets to sides of bag with bottom of pocket at Rnd 2. Sew center of strap to center back of bag where flap is attached. Sew ends of strap to base of bag. Sew one half of snap fastener to wrong side of flap and the other half to right side of bag. Sew button to right side of flap for decoration.

Market Tote

SUPPLIES

G6/4mm crochet hook

Small amount of DK, Light Worsted yarn in turquoise, red, rust, yellow & brown

4 buttons, 3/8"

Sewing thread

BAG

With turquoise, make a magic ring, ch 1.

Rnd 1: 6 sc in ring, pull ring closed tight (6 sts).

Rnd 2: 2 sc in each st around; change to yellow in last st. Place marker for beginning of rnd and move marker up as each rnd is completed (12 sts).

Rnd 3: *sc in next st, 2 sc in next st* 6 times; change to rust in last st (18 sts).

Rnd 4: *sc in next 2 sts, 2 sc in next st* 6 times (24 sts).

Rnd 5: *sc in next 3 sts, 2 sc in next st* 6 times; change to yellow in last st (30 sts).

Rnd 6: sc in each st around; change to turquoise in last st.

Rnds 7-8: sc in each st around; change to yellow in last st.

Rnd 9: sc in each st around; change to red in last st.

Rnds 10-11: sc in each st around; change to yellow in last st.

Rnd 12: sc in each st around; change to turquoise in last st.

Rnds 13-15: sc in each st around. Sl st in next st. Fasten off. Weave in ends.

HANDLES (MAKE 2)

With brown, ch 30.

Row 1: ch 1, turn, sc in each st across. Fasten off.

FINISHING

Sew 2 buttons to each side of bag spaced 1" apart as shown in photo. Tie tails of handle around one button. Pull a 12" piece of yarn through other end of handle (to make tails) and tie around next button. Weave ends through to wrong side. Repeat with 2nd handle on other side of bag.

Little Bow Purse

SUPPLIES

G6/4mm crochet hook

Small amount of DK, Light Worsted yarn

Note: A chain 1 at the beginning of a row is for turning your work and does not count as a stitch.

BAG

Ch 10.

Rows 1-17: ch 1, turn, sc in each st across (10 sts). Fasten off. Weave in ends. Fold rectangle in half widthwise.

STRAP

Join with sc at one lower corner of bag and sc in each st across (through both layers); ch for 8"; sc in each st across 2nd side of bag (through both layers). Fasten off. Weave in ends.

BOW

Ch 8.

Rows 1-4: ch 1, turn, sc in each st across (8 sts).

Fasten off. Weave in ends.

To make **center tie** for bow, ch 3, fasten off with long tail.

Pinch bow in middle and place tie over pinch so that chain portion of tie is in front of bow. Knot tie securely in place. Use tails to tie bow to purse. Sew each corner of bow to purse.

NIGHTWEAR

Pajamas

STAR APPLIQUE

Make a magic ring, ch 1.

Rnd 1: 10 sc in ring, pull ring closed tight, join with sl st in 1st sc.

Rnd 2: *ch 4, sc in 2nd ch from hook, hdc in next ch, dc in next ch, skip next st of Rnd 1, sl st in next st* 5 times. Fasten off. Pinch tips into nice points.

PAJAMA PANTS

The pants are made by alternating 2 rows of aqua with 2 rows of lavender. A slit is made at the back for the bunny's tail.

Note: A chain 1 at the beginning of a row is for turning your work and does not count as a stitch.

SIDE (MAKE 2)

With aqua, ch 20.

Rows 1-20: ch 1, turn, sc in each st across (20 sts). Change to alternate color in last st of every other row carrying the unused yarn along the edge. Fasten off.

FINISHING

Place pants pieces side-by-side with stripes vertical and edges with carried yarn at top. For **center front** seam, use invisible thread to sew top 10 sts together (see dotted line in photo below). For **center back** seam, sew top 2 sts together, skip next 5 sts, sew next 3 sts together. (The gap will make a slit for bunny's tail.) To form **legs**, sew first and last rows together on each side. For **waistband**, join lavender with sc at top and work a rnd of sc along edge, working over the carried yarn. Fasten off. Weave in ends. Thread a needle with elastic cord and weave through back of stitches around waistband. Try pants on bunny to get the right tension so it's not too loose or too tight. Tie a knot to secure elastic and weave in ends.

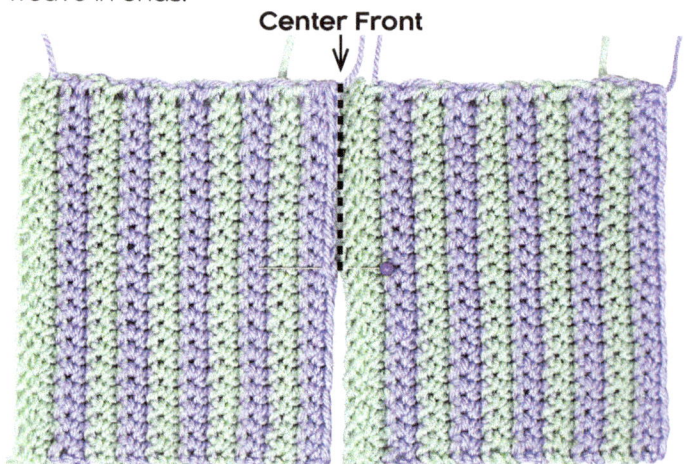

Center Front

SUPPLIES

G6/4mm crochet hook

Small amount of DK, Light Worsted yarn in aqua & lavender

Stretch Magic clear elastic bead cord (.7mm)

Invisible sewing thread

PAJAMA TOP

Follow instructions for Basic Shirt (see page 21) to make the PJ top. Make a heart or a star applique to sew on the front.

HEART APPLIQUE

Make a magic ring, ch 3. All sts except the chs are worked into the ring.

Rnd 1: 3 tr, 3 dc, tr, 3 dc, 3 tr, ch 3, sl st. Pull ring closed tight. Fasten off.

Carrot Sleeping Bag

Rnds 4-5: sc in each st around.

Rnd 6: *sc in next st, 2 sc in next st* 6 times (18 sts).

Rnds 7-8: sc in each st around.

Rnd 9: *sc in next 2 sts, 2 sc in next st* 6 times (24 sts).

Rnds 10-42: sc in each st around until 1 st remains, 2 sc in last st (57 sts at Rnd 42).

Fasten off. Weave in ends.

To make **front slit**, change to working in rows.

Row 1: join orange with sc at center front, sc in each st across (57 sts).

Rows 2-6: ch 1, turn, sc in each st across; change to green in last st.

Row 7: ch 1, turn, dc in each st across.

Row 8: ch 1, turn, 3 dc in each st across (171 sts).

Fasten off. Weave in ends.

FINISHING

For **tie**, make a 30" chain and weave it through the sts of Row 7. Trim tails to 1/2".

SUPPLIES

MEDIUM 4

H8/5mm crochet hook

100 yds of Worsted weight yarn in orange

30 yds of Worsted weight yarn in green

With orange, make a magic ring, ch 1.

Rnd 1: 6 sc in ring, pull ring closed tight (6 sts).

Rnd 2: sc in each st around. Place marker for beginning of rnd and move marker up as each rnd is completed.

Rnd 3: 2 sc in each st around (12 sts).

Garden Playmat

The delightful garden is designed so that little crocheted vegetables can be planted and picked. The root and tuber vegetables are planted in holes. They can be inserted on their side (see photo above) or standing up with the "soil" arranged around them for support (see photo next page). The surface-growing vegetables attach to the garden with hook and loop fasteners which make a fun noise when the veggies are picked!

Worsted weight yarn and hdc are used to make the top of the garden. Openings are made in the crochet for planting holes. The garden is backed with purchased fabric. Corduroy is ideal, or choose something with a similar weight.

SUPPLIES

H8/5mm crochet hook

240 yds of Worsted weight yarn in brown

1/2 yd of medium weight woven cotton fabric in brown

1/2 yd of 3/4" wide hook & loop fastener tape, hook side (rough side), in brown

Sewing thread in brown

SIZE 12" x 20"

Note: A chain 1 at the beginning of a row is for turning your work and does not count as a stitch.

With brown, ch 48.

Rows 1-6: ch 1, turn, hdc in each st across (48 sts).

In the next row, 5 openings are made for "planting" vegetables.

Row 7: ch 1, turn, hdc in first 2 sts, *ch 8, skip next 8 sts, hdc in next st* 5 times, hdc in last st (8 hdc, 40 ch).

Row 8: ch 1, turn, hdc in each hdc or ch across (48 sts).

Rows 9-22: ch 1, turn, hdc in each st across.

In the next row, 5 openings are made for "planting" vegetables.

Row 23: ch 1, turn, hdc in first 2 sts, *ch 8, skip next 8 sts, hdc in next st* 5 times, hdc in last st (8 hdc, 40 ch).

Row 24: ch 1, turn, hdc in each hdc or ch across (48 sts).

Rows 25-38: ch 1, turn, hdc in each st across.

In the next row, 5 openings are made for "planting" vegetables.

Row 39: ch 1, turn, hdc in first 2 sts, *ch 8, skip next 8 sts, hdc in next st* 5 times, hdc in last st (8 hdc, 40 ch).

Row 40: ch 1, turn, hdc in each hdc or ch across (48 sts).

Rows 41-54: ch 1, turn, hdc in each st across.

In the next row, 5 openings are made for "planting" vegetables.

Row 55: ch 1, turn, hdc in first 2 sts, *ch 8, skip next 8 sts, hdc in next st* 5 times, hdc in last st (8 hdc, 40 ch).

Row 56: ch 1, turn, hdc in each hdc or ch across (48 sts).

Rows 57-62: ch 1, turn, hdc in each st across.

Fasten off. Weave in ends.

FINISHING

Preshrink backing fabric by washing in hot water and machine drying. Lay crocheted garden on top of backing fabric. Cut fabric in a rectangle that is 1/2" larger than garden on all sides. Iron the 1/2" excess to the wrong side. Place garden and fabric with wrong sides facing and sew together around edges with whip stitch.

Sew across mat halfway between rows of holes (see dotted lines in photo below) sewing thru both layers so that the crocheted layer and the fabric backing are fastened together. You can sew by hand or with a sewing machine. I like to use a sewing machine for this.

Sew Here   Sew Here   Sew Here

Using a coin as a pattern (dime or penny), cut rough side of hook & loop fastener tape into 12 circles. Sew dots to mat halfway between rows of holes and evenly spaced as shown in photo below: sew thru all layers as you work making sure to catch the fabric backing in your stitches.

VEGETABLES

Traditional colors are used here for the vegetables, but all are grown in different varieties with different colors. This provides another opportunity to have fun with color.

Carrot

The carrot is worked from the top down. You can make it with or without the root—or make a variety. This little carrot fits nicely in Honey Bunny's pocket or purse. Make 5 carrots to fill the garden.

SUPPLIES

F5/3.75mm crochet hook

Small amount of DK, Light Worsted yarn in orange and green

Stuffing

CARROT

With orange, make a magic ring, ch 1.

Rnd 1: 5 sc in ring, pull ring closed tight (5 sts).

Rnd 2: 2 sc in each st around. Place marker for beginning of rnd and move marker up as each rnd is completed (10 sts).

Rnd 3: sc in each st around.

Rnd 4: sc in next 8 sts, sc2tog (9 sts).

Rnd 5: sc in next 7 sts, sc2tog (8 sts).

Rnd 6: sc in next 6 sts, sc2tog (7 sts).

Rnd 7: sc2tog, sc in next 2 sts, sc2tog, sc in next st (5 sts).

Fasten off. Stuff carrot, pushing in stuffing with tweezers. Thread ending tail onto needle, insert needle thru front loop of each stitch around opening and pull tight to close hole. Trim tail to 1/2 inch and separate plies for carrot root; or, for a rootless carrot, weave in end.

LEAVES

Cut four 6-inch strands of green. Sew a strand under sts of Rnd 1 across top of carrot. Pull ends until they meet. Repeat with other 3 strands at evenly spaced intervals. Cut an 8-inch strand of green, knot it tightly around base of leaves and sew tails into carrot to hide. Trim leaves to 1 inch.

Beet

Make 5 beets to fill the garden.

SUPPLIES

F5/3.75mm crochet hook

Small amount of DK, Light Worsted yarn in purple and green

Stuffing

BEET

With purple, make a magic ring, ch 1.

Rnd 1: 5 sc in ring, pull ring closed tight (5 sts).

Rnd 2: 2 sc in each st around. Place marker for beginning of rnd and move marker up as each rnd is completed (10 sts).

Rnd 3: *sc in next st, 2 sc in next st* 5 times (15 sts).

Rnd 4: *sc in next 2 sts, 2 sc in next st* 5 times (20 sts).

Rnds 5-7: sc in each st around.

Rnd 8: *sc in next 2 sts, sc2tog* 5 times (15 sts).

Rnd 9: *sc in next st, sc2tog* 5 times (10 sts).

Rnd 10: sc2tog 5 times (5 sts).

Fasten off. Stuff beet. Thread ending tail onto needle, insert needle thru front loop of each stitch around opening and pull tight to close hole. Trim tail to desired length for root and separate the plies.

LEAVES

With purple, ch 20, changing to green in last ch. Now work around this foundation chain.

Rnd 1: starting in 2nd ch from hook, sc in each ch around making 3 sts in same ch at each end.

Sl st in first st. Fasten off. Weave in ends. Knot a piece of green yarn around center and sew to beet. Hide ends.

Radish

Make 5 radishes to fill the garden.

SUPPLIES

F5/3.75mm crochet hook

Small amount of DK, Light Worsted yarn in red, green and white

Stuffing

RADISH

With red, make a magic ring, ch 1.

Rnd 1: 6 sc in ring, pull ring closed tight (6 sts).

Rnd 2: 2 sc in each st around. Place marker for beginning of rnd and move marker up as each rnd is completed (12 sts).

Rnd 3: *sc in next st, 2 sc in next st* 6 times (18 sts).

Rnds 4-6: sc in each st around.

Rnd 7: *sc in next st, sc2tog* 6 times (12 sts).

Rnd 8: sc2tog 6 times (6 sts).

Fasten off. To make root, thread needle with a short piece of white yarn and knot end. Insert needle into radish and out thru center of Rnd 1. Trim to desired length and separate plies.

Stuff radish. Thread red ending tail onto needle, insert needle thru front loop of each stitch around opening and pull tight to close hole. Weave in end.

LEAVES

For first leaf, ch 8 with green; 3 dc in 2nd ch from hook, sc in next st, sl st in next 5 sts (9 sts). Repeat twice more to make 2 more leaves.

Fasten off. Tie tails together, then use tails to sew leaves to top of radish. Hide ends.

Potato

Make 5 potatoes to fill the garden.

SUPPLIES

F5/3.75mm crochet hook

Small amount of DK, Light Worsted yarn in camel and brown

Stuffing

With camel, make a magic ring, ch 1.

Rnd 1: 6 sc in ring, pull ring closed tight (6 sts).

Rnd 2: 2 sc in each st around. Place marker for beginning of rnd and move marker up as each rnd is completed (12 sts).

Rnd 3: *sc in next 3 sts, 2 sc in next st* 3 times (15 sts).

Rnds 4-9: sc in each st around.

Rnd 10: *sc in next 3 sts, sc2tog* 3 times (12 sts).

Rnd 11: sc2tog 6 times (6 sts).

Sl st in next st. Fasten off. Stuff potato, pushing in stuffing with eraser end of new pencil. Thread ending tail onto needle, insert needle thru front loop of each stitch around opening and pull tight to close hole. Weave in end.

FINISHING

Thread yarn needle with a double strand of brown. Running needle back and forth thru potato, embroider small stitches in grooves between rnds to make the eyes: Pull tight as you make eyes to give potato a lumpy look. If eyes disappear into grooves, stitch over them again for more definition.

Cauliflower

Make 4 cauliflowers to fill the garden.

SUPPLIES

F5/3.75mm crochet hook

Small amount of DK, Light Worsted yarn in green and white

Stuffing

Small amount of 3/4" wide hook & loop fastener tape, loop side (soft side), in green

Sewing thread in green

HEAD

With white, make a magic ring, ch 1.

Rnd 1: 5 sc in ring, pull ring closed tight (5 sts).

Rnd 2: 2 sc in each st around. Place marker for beginning of rnd and move marker up as each rnd is completed (10 sts).

Rnd 3: *sc in next st, 2 sc in next st* 5 times (15 sts).

Rnd 4: sc in each st around.

Rnd 5: *sc in next st, sc2tog* 5 times (10 sts).

Rnd 6: sc2tog 5 times (5 sts).

Fasten off. Stuff cauliflower. Thread ending tail onto needle, insert needle thru front loop of each stitch around opening and pull tight to close hole. Weave in end.

LEAVES (MAKE 7)

With green, make a magic ring, ch 1.

Rnd 1: 5 sc in ring, pull ring closed tight (5 sts).

Rnd 2: 2 sc in each st around. Place marker for beginning of rnd and move marker up as each rnd is completed (10 sts).

Rnd 3: *sc in next st, 2 sc in next st* 5 times (15 sts).

Rnd 4: *sc in next 2 sts, 2 sc in next st* 5 times (20 sts).

Fasten off with extra long tail.

FINISHING

Using yarn tails, sew leaves to head in a staggered pattern (see photo) with **wrong side** of leaves facing head. Stab needle back and forth thru head to make stitches secure. Using a coin as a pattern (dime or penny), cut hook & loop fastener tape (soft side) into a circle. Sew dot to bottom of cauliflower.

Cabbage

Make cabbages the same as cauliflower using green yarn for head and leaves. Sew on leaves with **right side** facing head.

Pumpkin

Make 4 pumpkins to fill the garden.

SUPPLIES

F5/3.75mm crochet hook

Small amount of DK, Light Worsted yarn in orange and green

Stuffing

Small amount of 3/4" wide hook & loop fastener tape, loop side (soft side), in orange

Sewing thread in orange

PUMPKIN

With orange, make a magic ring, ch 1.

Rnd 1: 6 sc in ring, pull ring closed tight (6 sts).

Rnd 2: 2 sc in each st around. Place marker for beginning of rnd and move marker up as each rnd is completed (12 sts).

Rnd 3: *sc in next st, 2 sc in next st* 6 times (18 sts).

Rnd 4: *sc in next 2 sts, 2 sc in next st* 6 times (24 sts).

Rnd 5: *sc in next 3 sts, 2 sc in next st* 6 times (30 sts).

Rnds 6-10: sc in each st around.

Rnd 11: *sc in next 3 sts, sc2tog* 6 times (24 sts).

Rnd 12: *sc in next 2 sts, sc2tog* 6 times (18 sts).

Rnd 13: *sc in next st, sc2tog* 6 times (12 sts).

Rnd 14: sc2tog 6 times (6 sts).

Fasten off with extra long tail. Stuff pumpkin. To close hole, thread ending tail onto needle, insert needle thru front loop of each stitch around opening and pull tight. To shape pumpkin, push needle into bottom of pumpkin (Rnd 14) and out at top (Rnd 1); repeat and pull tight. This will make the first indentation. Do this 5 more times to make 6 evenly-spaced indentations. Weave in end securely.

LEAVES

With green, make a magic ring, ch 1.

Rnd 1: 8 sc in ring, pull ring closed tight (8 sts).

Rnd 2: *ch 3, skip next st, sl st in next st* 4 times.

Fasten off. Sew to top of pumpkin. Weave in ends.

STEM

With green, ch 5. Sc in 2nd ch from hook and in each remaining ch across. Fasten off. Sew to pumpkin at center of leaves. Hide ends.

FINISHING

Using a coin as a pattern (dime or penny), cut hook & loop fastener tape (soft side) into a circle. Sew dot to bottom of pumpkin pushing a small bit of stuffing under the dot as you sew.

GARDEN ACCESSORIES

Basket

The basket is worked in the round from the bottom up.

SUPPLIES

G6/4mm crochet hook

45 yds of Worsted weight yarn in gold

Make a magic ring, ch 1.

Rnd 1: 6 sc in ring, pull ring closed tight (6 sts).

Rnd 2: 2 sc in each st around. Place marker for beginning of rnd and move marker up as each rnd is completed (12 sts).

Rnd 3: *sc in next st, 2 sc in next st* 6 times (18 sts).

Rnd 4: *sc in next 2 sts, 2 sc in next st* 6 times (24 sts).

Rnd 5: *sc in next 3 sts, 2 sc in next st* 6 times (30 sts).

Rnd 6: *sc in next 4 sts, 2 sc in next st* 6 times (36 sts).

Rnd 7: *sc in next 5 sts, 2 sc in next st* 6 times (42 sts).

Rnd 8: *sc in next 6 sts, 2 sc in next st* 6 times (48 sts).

Rnd 9: working in **back loops only,** sc in each st around.

Rnds 10-19: resuming work in both loops, sc in each st around.

Rnd 20: *sc in next 18 sts; for **handle**, ch 8, skip next 6 sts* twice (36 sts, 16 ch).

Rnd 21: sc in each st or ch around (52 sts).

St st in next st. Fasten off. Weave in ends.

Sprinkling Can

The sprinkling can is worked in the round from the bottom up.

SUPPLIES

G6/4mm crochet hook

Small amount of Worsted weight yarn in yellow and blue

Stuffing

CAN

With yellow, make a magic ring, ch 1.

Rnd 1: 6 sc in ring, pull ring closed tight (6 sts).

Rnd 2: 2 sc in each st around. Place marker for beginning of rnd and move marker up as each rnd is completed (12 sts).

Rnd 3: *sc in next st, 2 sc in next st* 6 times (18 sts).

Rnd 4: *sc in next 2 sts, 2 sc in next st* 6 times (24 sts).

Rnd 5: working in **back loops only**, sc in each st around.

Rnds 6-14: resuming work in both loops, sc in each st around.

Rnd 15: working in **back loops only**, *sc in next 2 sts, sc2tog* 6 times; change to blue in last st (18 sts).

Rnd 16: resuming work in both loops, *sc in next st, sc2tog* 6 times (12 sts).

Rnd 17: sc2tog 6 times (6 sts).

Fasten off. Stuff cylinder.

Thread ending tail onto needle, insert needle thru front loop of each stitch around opening and pull tight to close hole.

BOTTOM RIM

With yellow, turn watering can upside down and crochet in unworked front loops of Rnd 5.

Rnd 1: sc in each st around (24 sts).

Rnd 2: sl st in each st around. Fasten off.

SPOUT

With yellow, make a magic ring, ch 1.

Rnd 1: 6 sc in ring, pull ring closed tight (6 sts).

Rnd 2: 2 sc in each st around. Place marker for beginning of rnd and move marker up as each rnd is completed (12 sts).

Rnd 3: working in **back loops only,** sc in each st around.

Rnd 4: resuming work in both loops, *sc in next st, sc2tog* 4 times (8 sts).

Rnd 5: sc in next 6 sts, sc2tog (7 sts).

Rnds 6-9: sc in each st around.

Rnd 10: sl st in next st, sc in next st, hdc in next 3 sts, sc in next st, sl st in last st (7 sts). Fasten off. Stuff spout.

HANDLE

With yellow, make a magic ring, ch 1.

Rnd 1: 5 sc in ring, pull ring closed tight (5 sts).

Rnds 2-25: sc in each st around. Fasten off.

FINISHING

Sew spout and handle to sprinkling can referring to photos for placement. Weave in ends.

Compost Bucket

The compost bucket is worked in the round from the bottom up. The handle attaches to the bucket with buttons so that it is movable.

SUPPLIES

MEDIUM 4

G6/4mm crochet hook

Small amount of Worsted weight yarn in green and brown

2 buttons, 3/8"

Sewing thread

Stuffing

BUCKET

With green, make a magic ring, ch 1.

Rnd 1: 6 sc in ring, pull ring closed tight (6 sts).

Rnd 2: 2 sc in each st around. Place marker for beginning of rnd and move marker up as each rnd is completed (12 sts).

Rnd 3: *sc in next st, 2 sc in next st* 6 times (18 sts).

Rnd 4: *sc in next 2 sts, 2 sc in next st* 6 times (24 sts).

Rnd 5: working in **back loops only,** sc in each st around.

Rnds 6-14: resuming work in both loops, sc in each st around; change to brown in last st.

Rnd 15: working in **back loops only,** *sc in next 2 sts, sc2tog* 6 times (18 sts).

Rnd 16: resuming work in both loops, *sc in next st, sc2tog* 6 times (12 sts).

Rnd 17: sc2tog 6 times (6 sts).

Fasten off. Stuff the bucket. Thread ending tail onto needle, insert needle thru front loop of each stitch around opening and pull tight to close hole.

BOTTOM RIM

With green, turn bucket upside down and crochet in unworked front loops of Rnd 5.

Rnd 1: sc in each st around (24 sts).

Rnd 2: sl st in each st around. Fasten off.

HANDLE

With green, ch 23. For **buttonhole**, skip first 5 chs from hook, sc in last 18 chs; for second **buttonhole**, ch 4, fasten off and tie tails together. Weave in ends.

FINISHING

Sew a button to each side of bucket at the upper edge (see photo). Button handle to bucket. Weave in ends.

Shovel

A dab of glue keeps a wooden skewer inside the handle from poking thru the crochet during play.

SUPPLIES

MEDIUM 4

G6/4mm crochet hook

Small amount of Worsted weight yarn in gray and red

1 wooden skewer

White glue

BLADE

With gray, make a magic ring, ch 1.

Rnd 1: 6 sc in ring, pull ring closed tight (6 sts).

Rnd 2: sc in each st around. Place marker for beginning of rnd and move marker up as each rnd is completed.

Rnd 3: 2 sc in each st around (12 sts).

Rnd 4: sc in each st around.

Rnd 5: *sc in next st, 2 sc in next st* 6 times (18 sts).

Rnds 6-9: sc in each st around. Fasten off.

HANDLE

With red, make a magic ring, ch 1.

Rnd 1: 6 sc in ring, pull ring closed tight (6 sts).

Rnds 2-15: sc in each st around; change to gray in last st. Place marker for beginning of rnd and move marker up as each rnd is completed.

Rnds 16-21: sc in each st around. Fasten off.

FINISHING

Dip blunt end of skewer in white glue and scrape off the excess. Insert blunt end in handle and cut to fit length of tube. Sew open end of handle shut. Flatten blade and put gray end of handle centered inside. Sew open edge of blade closed— sewing handle to blade as you work. Weave in ends.

HONEY BUNNY'S GARDEN FRIENDS

Ladybug

The ladybug is worked in the round.

SUPPLIES

F5/3.75mm crochet hook

Small amount of DK, Light Worsted yarn in red and black

2 pearl beads, 3mm

3 black buttons, 3/8"

Stuffing

Sewing thread in black

BOTTOM

With black, make a magic ring, ch 1.

Rnd 1: 6 sc in ring, pull ring closed tight (6 sts).

Rnd 2: 2 sc in each st around. Place marker for beginning of rnd and move marker up as each rnd is completed (12 sts).

Rnd 3: *sc in next st, 2 sc in next st* 6 times (18 sts).

Rnd 4: *sc in next 2 sts, 2 sc in next st* 6 times (24 sts).

Fasten off.

TOP

With red, make a magic ring, ch 1.

Rnd 1: 6 sc in ring, pull ring closed tight (6 sts).

Rnd 2: 2 sc in each st around. Place marker for beginning of rnd and move marker up as each rnd is completed (12 sts).

Rnd 3: *sc in next st, 2 sc in next st* 6 times (18 sts).

Rnd 4: *sc in next 2 sts, 2 sc in next st* 6 times (24 sts).

Rnds 5-6: sc in each st around.

Do not fasten off. Place bottom and top with wrong sides facing and match them up stitch for stitch. Sc the pieces together. Stuff ladybug when a small hole remains, then finish connecting. Fasten off. Weave in ends.

HEAD

With black, make a magic ring, ch 1.

Rnd 1: 6 sc in ring, pull ring closed tight (6 sts).

Rnd 2: 2 sc in each st around (12 sts).

Fasten off.

FINISHING

Sew head in place as shown in photos . Weave in ends. For eyes, sew beads to head in groove between Rnds 1-2 so that they are level with middle. Sew buttons evenly spaced to top of ladybug.

Bee

The bee is worked in the round.

SUPPLIES

LIGHT 3

F5/3.75mm crochet hook

Small amount of DK, Light Worsted yarn in yellow, black and white

2 black beads, 4mm

Stuffing

Sewing thread in black and white

BODY

With yellow, make a magic ring, ch 1.

Rnd 1: 6 sc in ring, pull ring closed tight (6 sts).

Rnd 2: 2 sc in each st around. Place marker for beginning of rnd and move marker up as each rnd is completed (12 sts).

Rnd 3: *sc in next st, 2 sc in next st* 6 times (18 sts).

Rnd 4: sc in each st around; change to black in last st.

Rnd 5: sc in each st around.

Rnd 6: sc in each st around; change to yellow in last st.

Rnd 7: sc in each st around.

Rnd 8: sc in each st around; change to black in last st.

Rnd 9: sc in each st around.

Rnd 10: sc in each st around; change to yellow in last st.

Rnd 11: sc in each st around.

Rnd 12: *sc in next st, sc2tog* 6 times; change to black in last st (12 sts).

Rnd 13: sc2tog around (6 sts).

Fasten off. Stuff bee. Thread ending tail onto needle, insert needle thru front loop of each stitch around opening and pull tight to close hole.

WINGS

With white, make a magic ring, ch 1.

Rnd 1: 6 sc in ring, pull ring closed just until you have a half circle with one straight side (6 sts).

Fasten off.

FINISHING

Place flat side of wings against top of body on middle yellow stripe. Sew in place with thread spaced 1/2" apart using photo as a guide. For eyes, sew on beads so that they are level with middle of face. Weave in ends.

Earthworm

The earthworm is made to hold a pose with an optional pipe cleaner inside.

SUPPLIES

LIGHT 3

F5/3.75mm crochet hook

Small amount of DK, Light Worsted yarn in raspberry

2 black beads, 4mm

1 chenille pipe cleaner (optional)

Stuffing

Sewing thread in black

Beginning at head, make a magic ring, ch 1.

Rnd 1: 8 sc in ring, pull ring closed tight (8 sts).

Rnds 2-3: sc in each st around. Place marker for beginning of rnd and move marker up as each rnd is completed.

Rnd 4: sc2tog twice, sc in next 4 sts (6 sts).

Rnds 5-23: sc in each st around.

With eraser end of a new pencil, push stuffing into head only; do not stuff body. Insert pipe cleaner in worm cutting pipe cleaner to match length of worm.

Rnd 24: sc2tog 3 times (3 sts).

Fasten off. Weave in end.

FINISHING

For eyes, sew beads to sides of head.

Snail

The snail shell is worked with 2 strands of yarn in different colors held together. If you've never crocheted with multiple strands, just pretend you are working with a single strand and make each stitch as if you were holding one strand of yarn. That's really all there is to it.

SUPPLIES

F5/3.75mm crochet hook

Small amount of DK, Light Worsted yarn in blue, brown and tan

Stuffing

2 black beads, 3mm

Sewing thread in black

LIGHT 3

BODY

With blue, make a magic ring, ch 1.

Rnd 1: 5 sc in ring, pull ring closed tight (5 sts).

Rnd 2: 2 sc in each st around. Place marker for beginning of rnd and move marker up as each rnd is completed (10 sts).

Rnd 3: sc in each st around.

Rnd 4: to make **upper tentacles,** *sc in next 2 sts, ch 4, sl st in 2nd ch from hook, sl st in next 2 ch* twice, sc in next 6 sts (10 sts).

For next rnd, you will need to pass behind each tentacle to reach next st.

Rnds 5-15: sc in each st around.

Rnd 16: *sc in next 3 sts, sc2tog* twice (8 sts).

Rnd 17: sc in each st around. Stuff body softly.

Rnd 18: *sc in next 2 sts, sc2tog* twice (6 sts).

Rnd 19: *sc in next st, sc2tog* twice (4 sts).

Fasten off. Weave in end.

SHELL (MAKE 2)

With 1 strand of brown and 1 strand of tan held together, make a magic ring, ch 1.

Rnd 1: 6 sc in ring (6 sts).

Rnd 2: 2 sc in each st around. Place marker for beginning of rnd and move marker up as each rnd is completed (12 sts).

Rnd 3: *sc in next st, 2 sc in next st* around (18 sts).

Rnds 4-5: sc in each st around.

Slip st in next st. Fasten off.

FINISHING

Place shell pieces with wrong sides facing and sew them together by going under the sts of Rnd 5. Stuff shell when a small hole remains, then finish connecting. Weave in ends. Place shell at center top of body with the point of fastening off against body. Sew shell in place with blue yarn by pushing needle up from bottom of body thru top of shell and back down again. Repeat several times making sure to bring your needle up and down between halves of shell so that sewing yarn is hidden. For **lower tentacle**, ch 3, sl st in 2nd ch from hook and in next ch. Fasten off. Repeat for 2nd tentacle. Sew tentacles to sides of face. Weave in ends. For eyes, sew beads to top of upper tentacles.

Banana Slug

SUPPLIES

F5/3.75mm crochet hook

Small amount of DK, Light Worsted yarn in yellow

Stuffing

2 black beads, 3mm

Sewing thread in black

Make a magic ring, ch 1.

Rnd 1: 5 sc in ring, pull ring closed tight (5 sts).

Rnd 2: 2 sc in each st around. Place marker for beginning of rnd and move marker up as each rnd is completed (10 sts).

Rnd 3: sc in each st around.

Rnd 4: for **upper tentacles**, *sc in next 2 sts, ch 4, sc in 2nd ch from hook, sl st in next 2 ch* twice, sc in next 6 sts (10 sts).

For next rnd, you will need to pass behind each tentacle to reach next st.

Rnds 5-18: sc in each st around.

Rnd 19: *sc in next 3 sts, sc2tog* twice (8 sts).

Rnd 20: sc in each st around. Stuff slug.

Rnd 21: *sc in next 2 sts, sc2tog* twice (6 sts).

Rnd 22: *sc in next st, sc2tog* twice (4 sts).

Fasten off. Weave in end.

FINISHING

For **lower tentacle**, ch 3, sl st in 2nd ch from hook and in next ch. Fasten off. Repeat for 2nd tentacle. Sew to sides of face. Weave in ends. For eyes, sew beads to top of upper tentacles.

Garden Spider

The spider is worked from the back of the body toward the head. The legs are stiffened with clear-drying white glue. Your favorite brand will do fine.

SUPPLIES

F5/3.75mm crochet hook

Small amount of DK, Light Worsted yarn in camel

2 black beads, 3mm

All purpose white craft glue

Stuffing

Sewing thread in black

BODY & HEAD

Make a magic ring, ch 1.

Rnd 1: 6 sc in ring, pull ring closed tight (6 sts).

Rnd 2: 2 sc in each st around. Place marker for beginning of rnd and move marker up as each rnd is completed (12 sts).

Rnds 3-6: sc in each st around.

Rnd 7: sc2tog 6 times (6 sts).

Rnd 8: for **head**, *sc in next st, 2 sc in next st* 3 times (9 sts).

Rnd 9: sc in each st around.

Rnd 10: sc in first st, sc2tog 4 times (5 sts).

Fasten off. Stuff spider. Thread ending tail onto needle, insert needle thru front loop of each stitch around opening and pull tight to close hole. To define head better, tie a piece of yarn between Rnds 7-8 and knot securely. Do not weave in these ends as they will later be used to tie legs to body.

LEGS (MAKE 4)

Note: Each leg strand will become 2 legs.

Ch 21 tightly. Fasten off. Grasp chain by the tails and pull firmly to tighten the knots. Trim tails a short distance from knots.

Bottom Side

FINISHING

Squeeze a line of glue along underside of each leg strand. Rub glue with your finger to blend it into yarn. Bend strands into crescent shapes and let dry. Stack 2 strands curving frontward and 2 strands curving backward. Using reserved yarn tails at spider's neck, tie around center of leg strands. For eyes, sew beads to sides of head. Weave in ends.

Caterpillar

SUPPLIES

F5/3.75mm crochet hook

Small amount of DK, Light Worsted yarn in green, black and yellow

2 black beads, 3mm

Sewing thread in black

Stuffing

LIGHT 3

With green, make a magic ring, ch 1.

Rnd 1: 5 sc in ring, pull ring closed tight (5 sts).

Rnd 2: 2 sc in each st around. Place marker for beginning of rnd and move marker up as each rnd is completed (10 sts).

Rnd 3: sc in each st around; change to black in last st.

Rnd 4: sc in each st around; change to green in last st.

Rnds 5-8: sc in each st around; change to black in last st.

Rnd 9: sc in each st around; change to green in last st.

Rnds 10-13: sc in each st around; change to black in last st.

Rnd 14: sc in each st around; change to green in last st.

Rnds 15-18: sc in each st around; change to black in last st.

Rnd 19: sc in each st around; change to green in last st.

Rnds 20-21: sc in each st around. Stuff caterpillar.

Rnd 22: sc2tog 5 times (5 sts).

Fasten off. Thread ending tail onto needle, insert needle thru front loop of each stitch around opening and pull tight to close hole. Weave in end.

FINISHING

Thread needle with a double strand of black yarn; wrap it around caterpillar between each pair of black stripes, pulling yarn to make an indentation and securing with a stitch. (Push needle thru center of caterpillar to location for each new stripe.) Hide ends inside. With a double strand of yellow, embroider small stitches on black rnds as shown in photo. For eyes, sew beads in groove between Rnds 2-3 so that they are level with middle of face. ♥

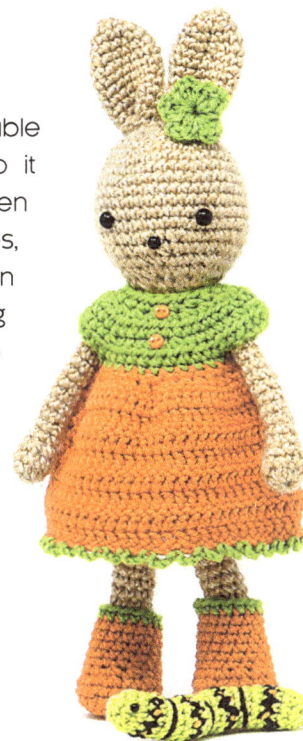

Stitches

SLIP KNOT

This is used to make a starting loop on the crochet hook.

1. Make a loop about 5 inches from end of yarn. Insert hook in loop and hook onto supply yarn (yarn coming from ball) at A.

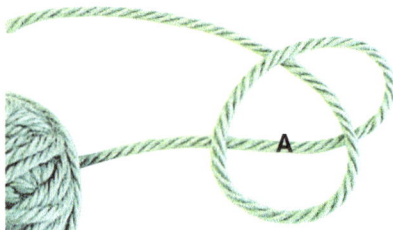

2. Pull yarn through loop.

3. Pull yarn ends to tighten loop around hook.

SLIP STITCH (SL ST)

1. Insert hook in stitch. Yarn over and pull through stitch and through loop on hook (A and B).

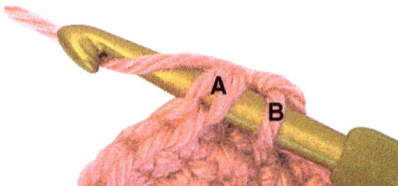

2. The sl st is done.

CHAIN (CH)

Start with a slip knot on hook.

1. Bring yarn **over** hook from back to front. Catch yarn with hook and pull it through the loop —

to look like this. One ch is done.

SINGLE CROCHET (SC)

This simple stitch is the primary stitch for amigurumi.

1. Insert hook in designated stitch. Note: Put hook under **both loops** that form v-shape at top of stitch unless otherwise instructed.

2. Yarn over and pull through the stitch (A).

You now have 2 loops on the hook:

3. Yarn over and pull through both loops on hook.

4. You now have 1 loop on hook and the sc stitch is done.

HALF DOUBLE CROCHET (HDC)

1. Yarn over and insert hook in designated stitch.

2. Yarn over and pull through the stitch (A).

You now have 3 loops on hook:

3. Yarn over and pull through all 3 loops on hook (A, B & C).

4. You now have 1 loop on hook and the hdc stitch is done.

DOUBLE CROCHET (DC)

1. Yarn over and insert hook in designated stitch.

2. Yarn over and pull through the stitch (A).

You now have 3 loops on hook:

3. Yarn over and pull through 1st 2 loops on hook (A and B).

You now have 2 loops on hook:

4. Yarn over and pull through both loops on hook.

5. You now have 1 loop on hook and the dc stitch is done.

TRIPLE OR TREBLE CROCHET (TR)

1. Yarn over twice, insert hook into stitch.

2. Yarn over and pull yarn through, bringing up a loop.

3. Yarn over again and pull yarn through the **first two loops** on the hook.

4. Yarn over again and pull yarn through the **next two loops** on the hook.

5. Yarn over again and pull yarn through the **last two loops** on the hook.

6. You now have 1 loop on hook and the tr stitch is done.

SINGLE CROCHET DECREASE (SC2TOG)

The instruction "sc2tog" means to use single crochet to join 2 stitches together. It is a way to decrease or make the item smaller.

1. Insert hook in stitch, yarn over and pull up a loop — to look like this:

2. Insert hook in next stitch, yarn over and pull up a loop — to look like this:

3. Yarn over and pull through all 3 loops on hook — to look like this. The sc2tog is done.

DOUBLE CROCHET DECREASE (DC2TOG)

1. Yarn over, insert hook in st and pull up a loop.

2. Yarn over and pull through 2 loops.

3. Yarn over, insert hook in next st and pull up a loop.

4. Yarn over, pull through 2 loops.

5. Yarn over and pull through all loops on hook.

6. You now have 1 loop on your hook and the dc2tog is done.

Techniques

★ MAGIC RING

Most all of my amigurumi begins with the magic ring. This is an adjustable loop that makes a neat center when crocheting in the round. If you're not familiar with it, you may want to watch a YouTube tutorial. It's not difficult — and well worth it.

An alternative to the magic ring, if desired, is to ch 2; then begin Rnd 1 by working the required number of sts as stated in the pattern into the 2nd ch from the hook, This method will leave a small hole in the middle of the first round (see photo below).

Magic Ring   Ch 2

Make the Magic Ring as follows:

1. Make a ring a few inches from end of yarn. Grasp ring between thumb and index finger where the join makes an X. Insert hook in ring, hook onto supply yarn at Y and pull up a loop —

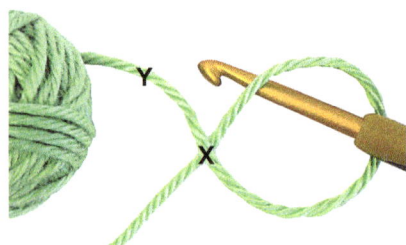

to look like this.

2. Chain 1 —

to look like this. This chain does not count as a stitch.

3. Insert hook into ring so you're crocheting over ring and yarn tail. Pull up a loop to begin your first single crochet —

and complete the single crochet.

4. Continue to crochet over ring and yarn tail for the specified number of single crochets for the 1st round.

5. Pull tail to close up ring. To begin the 2nd round, insert hook in 1st stitch of 1st round (see arrow).

BEGIN 2ND RND HERE

WORKING IN THE ROUND

Working in the round means crocheting in a continuous spiral. Most amigurumi is worked this way.

WORKING IN LOOPS

When a single crochet stitch is made, you will see 2 loops in a v-shape at the top of the stitch. To crochet the patterns in this book, insert your hook under **both loops** unless instructed otherwise. Crocheting in the "front loops only" or the "back loops only" is sometimes used for a different effect.

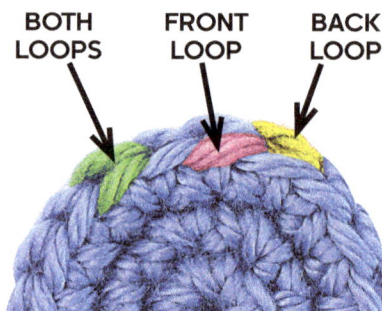

BOTH   FRONT   BACK
LOOPS   LOOP   LOOP

CHANGING COLORS

To change color while single crocheting, work last stitch of old color to last yarn over, yarn over with new color and pull through both loops to complete the stitch.

ROTATING YOUR HOOK

When you wrap yarn over your hook, the front of the hook should be facing you. Then when it's time to pull the yarn through the loop on the hook, rotate the hook downward. It will slide easily through the loop instead of getting caught.

COUNTING ROUNDS

Periodically, it is good to count your rounds to ensure your place in a pattern. Fortunately, rounds are clearly defined and counting is easy. Each round makes a ridge. A groove separates the rounds. You need only to count the ridges. Take a look at the photo below to see that the circle has 5 rounds.

USING STITCH MARKERS

It can be tricky to keep track of your place when working in the round, so be sure to use a stitch marker. Place the stitch marker in the first stitch of a round — after completing the stitch. When you've crocheted all the way around, remove the stitch marker, make the next stitch, and replace the marker in the stitch just made. This will be the first stitch of the next round.

RUNNING STITCH MARKER

Stitch markers are essential in amigurumi to mark specific spots on your work. You can use one any time you feel it is necessary and sometimes the pattern will indicate that a marker is needed. A Running Stitch Marker is a scrap of yarn in a contrasting color that is woven back and forth between rounds. I especially like this type of marker for narrow cylinders such as arms and legs.

When you complete your first round, lay your "marker-yarn" over your work before starting the next round. Then when you work the first stitch of the next round, the yarn will be trapped between the stitches. At the end of each successive round, fold the marker-yarn back over your work: if it's in the back, fold it to the front, if it's in the front, fold it to the back. This way the yarn is flipped back and forth—between the last stitch of each round and the first stitch of the next round. When you're done, simply pull the marker-yarn out.

FASTENING OFF

This is the way to finish a piece so that it won't unravel. When you're done crocheting, cut the yarn and leave a tail. Wrap the tail over your hook and pull it all the way through the last loop left on your hook. Pull the tail tight and it will make a knot.

SMOOTHING THE EDGE

When fastening off, the knot can make a small bump in the edge of your work so that, for example, a round shape will not look as round as it should. To make the edge smooth, thread the long tail in a yarn needle and insert the needle down through the center "V" of the next stitch. This little step makes a big difference!

JOINING WITH SC

Put yarn on hook with a Slip Knot. Insert hook in indicated stitch. Complete sc as shown in Single Crochet tutorial, page 60, steps 2-4.

JOINING WITH SL ST

Start with a Slip Knot on hook. Insert hook in specified stitch. Yarn over and pull through the stitch and the loop on the hook.

ASSEMBLING

The assembly stage of amigurumi is an exciting time. This is when various pieces are sewn together and the project blossoms in cuteness! Thread a yarn needle with the tail of your auxiliary piece (ear, arm, leg, etc.) and use a whip stitch or running stitch to sew it in place. You may want to pin your pieces in place beforehand to be sure the position looks good. A sewing needle and thread can also be used to sew your parts together. In some cases, this will make the stitches less visible.

WEAVING IN ENDS

The assembly of every pattern includes the instruction to weave in the ends. This is the way to hide and secure all of your straggly yarn tails. Thread the yarn end into a yarn needle, then skim through the back of the stitches on the wrong side of your work. Continue for about 2 inches, then turn and double back to lock the yarn into place. Trim the end close. When you turn your work to the right side, you should not see the woven ends. They should be tucked into the middle of your crocheted fabric.

ADDING WIRE

If your bunny is made for display, not for play, you can insert wire in the arms, legs or both so that it will hold a pose. This will make your bunny more like an action figure than a cuddly stuffie. Use a heavy wire of 16 to 19 gauge. Begin when the bunny's head and body are stuffed and connected.

Stuff the arm or leg as instructed in the pattern, but you will have to work the stuffing in around the wire.

For the arms, cut a 9" piece of wire.

1. Bend one end into a small loop with needle-nose pliers and insert into first arm through to hand.

2. Insert exposed end of wire into body where the arm will be placed.

3. Push wire all the way through body to opposite side where you will sew the other arm.

4. Bend exposed tip of wire into a small loop and insert into 2nd arm.

5. Sew both arms to body around wire core.

For the legs, cut two 9" pieces of wire. Note: You will have to keep the ends of the legs open, omitting the bunny pattern's instruction to close top of leg with sc.

1. Bend one end into a small loop and insert into first leg through to foot.

2. Insert exposed end of wire into body where the leg will be placed.

3. Push wire all the way through body and into head.

4. Repeat for second leg.

5. Sew both legs to body around wire core.

FRENCH KNOT

Bring needle up from wrong side at A. Place needle close to fabric and wrap yarn around needle 2 or 3 times. Push needle down at a point near A.

A

SAFETY

Most packaging for plastic animal eyes has the following warning: "Contains small parts that may present a choking hazard for children under 3". If the bunny is for a child under age 3, embroidery or small felt circles can be used as alternatives to plastic eyes.

Resources

YARN

Amazon
amazon.com

Herrschners
herrschners.com

Joann Fabric and Craft Stores
joann.com

NOTIONS

Amazon
amazon.com

Joann Fabric and Craft Stores
joann.com

ANIMAL EYES

Amazon
amazon.com

CR's Crafts
crscrafts.com

Etsy Shop 6060
etsy.com/shop/6060

HOOK & LOOP FASTENER TAPE

Seattle Fabrics
seattlefabrics.com

VIDEO TUTORIALS

You Tube
youtube.com
Search on the name of the stitch or technique you want to learn.

Pinterest
pinterest.com/LindalooEnt/
Visit my Pinterest page to view video tutorials for the stitches and techniques used in this book. Look for the board named "Amigurumi Tutorials".

Yarn

Honey Bunny (Worsted, #4)
Lion Brand "Heartland", Sand Dunes

Basic Dress (DK, Light Worsted, #3)
Loops & Threads "Joy DK", Blossom

Rainbow Dress (DK, Light Worsted, #3)
Red Heart "Baby Hugs Light", Lilac
Lion Brand "Vanna's Style", Denim
Premier "Primo", Turquoise
Red Heart "Fashion Soft", Kelly Green
Red Heart "Fashion Soft", Flax
Red Heart "Baby Hugs Light", Orangie
Bergere de France "Barisienne", Vitelotte

Watermelon Dress (DK, Light Worsted, #3)
Red Heart "Baby Hugs Light", Peachie
Red Heart "Baby Hugs Light", Shell
Herrschners "Baby Yarn", Meadow
Red Heart "Fashion Soft", Black

Carrot Dress (DK, Light Worsted, #3)
Red Heart "Baby Hugs Light", Orangie
Herrschners "Kids' Brites", Grasshopper

Bumblebee Dress (DK, Light Worsted, #3)
Herrschners "Baby Yarn", Smile
Red Heart "Fashion Soft", Black

Ladybug Dress (DK, Light Worsted, #3)
Bergere de France "Barisienne", Vitelotte
Red Heart "Fashion Soft", Black

Pocket Dress (DK, Light Worsted, #3)
Loops & Threads "Joy DK", Lavender
Loops & Threads "Joy DK", Iris

Checked Dress (DK, Light Worsted, #3)
Lion Brand "Vanna's Style", Sky
Premier "Primo", Cream

Garden Fairy (DK, Light Worsted, #3)
Herrschners "Kids' Brites", Grasshopper
Herrschners "Baby Yarn", Meadow

Underwear (DK, Light Worsted, #3)
Red Heart "Baby Hugs Light", Sky

Overalls, Overall Dress, Jeans, Jeans Shorts
(DK, Light Worsted, #3)
Red Heart "Vanna's Style", Denim
Red Heart "Vanna's Style", Camel

Pajamas (DK, Light Worsted, #3)
Premier "Primo", Celery
Loops & Threads "Joy DK", Lavender

Basic Shirt (DK, Light Worsted, #3)
Loops & Threads "Joy DK", Lavender

Carrot Applique Shirt (DK, Light Worsted, #3)
Stylecraft "Special DK", Parchment
Red Heart "Baby Hugs Light", Orangie
Red Heart "Fashion Soft", Kelly Green

Flower Applique Shirt (DK, Light Worsted, #3)
Red Heart "Baby Hugs Light", Sunny
Bernat "Softee Baby", Soft Red

Collar Shirt (DK, Light Worsted, #3)
Stylecraft "Special DK", Cypress

Checked Shirt (DK, Light Worsted, #3)
Loops & Threads "Joy DK", Blossom
Loops & Threads "Joy DK", Spearmint
Bergere de France "Barisienne", Vitelotte
Bergere de France "Barisienne", Dolmen

Captain Compost (DK, Light Worsted, #3)
Red Heart "Fashion Soft", Kelly Green
Red Heart "Fashion Soft", Chocolate
Red Heart "Fashion Soft", Flax

Shorts (DK, Light Worsted, #3)
Loops & Threads "Joy DK", Blossom

Cargo Shorts (DK, Light Worsted, #3)
Red Heart "Fashion Soft", Flax

Pants (DK, Light Worsted, #3)
Red Heart "Fashion Soft", Nutmeg

Scarf (DK, Light Worsted, #3)
Lion Brand "Baby Soft", Pistachio
Premier "Primo", Peach

Gardening Hat (DK, Light Worsted, #3)
Red Heart "Vanna's Style", Camel
Red Heart "Fashion Soft", Chocolate

Beanie (DK, Light Worsted, #3)
Loops & Threads "Snuggly Wuggly", Blue Yonder

Cardigan (DK, Light Worsted, #3)
Loops & Threads "Snuggly Wuggly", Dove Gray

Gardening Apron (DK, Light Worsted, #3)
Red Heart "Baby Hugs Light", Orangie
Herrschners "Kids' Brites", Grasshopper
Red Heart "Fashion Soft", Chocolate

Backpack (DK, Light Worsted, #3)
Loops & Threads "Snuggly Wuggly", Dove Gray
Herrschners "Baby Yarn", Aqua

Market Tote (DK, Light Worsted, #3)
Loops & Threads "Joy DK", Spearmint
Red Heart "Fashion Soft", Flax
Red Heart "Fashion Soft", Chocolate
Red Heart "Fashion Soft", Nutmeg
Bergere de France "Barisienne", Vitelotte

Shoes (DK, Light Worsted, #3)
Loops & Threads "Snuggly Wuggly", Candy Pink
Herrschners "Kids' Brites", Grasshopper
Red Heart "Fashion Soft", Black

Sneakers (DK, Light Worsted, #3)
Stylecraft "Special DK", Plum
Red Heart "Fashion Soft", Flax
Red Heart "Baby Hugs Light", Bluie
Red Heart "Baby Hugs Light", Shell
Loops & Threads "Snuggly Wuggly", Candy Pink

Work Boots (DK, Light Worsted, #3)
Red Heart "Vanna's Style", Camel
Red Heart "Baby Hugs Light", Shell
Red Heart "Fashion Soft", Chocolate

Boots (DK, Light Worsted, #3)
Red Heart "Baby Hugs Light", Lilac
Red Heart "Baby Hugs Light", Orangie
Red Heart "Fashion Soft", Kelly Green

Carrot Sleeping Bag (Worsted, #4)
Red Heart "Soft", Tangerine
Red Heart "Soft", Guacamole

Garden (Worsted, #4)
Lion Brand "Heartland", Sequoia

Potato (DK, Light Worsted, #3)
Stylecraft "Special DK", Camel
Red Heart "Fashion Soft", Chocolate

Beet (DK, Light Worsted, #3)
Stylecraft "Special DK", Plum
Stylecraft "Special DK", Cypress

Radish (DK, Light Worsted, #3)
Bergere de France "Barisienne", Vitelotte
Stylecraft "Special DK", Meadow
Premier "Primo", Cream

Carrot (DK, Light Worsted, #3)
Red Heart "Baby Hugs Light", Orangie
Herrschners "Kids' Brites", Grasshopper

Cauliflower (DK, Light Worsted, #3)
Red Heart "Baby Hugs Light", Shell
Stylecraft "Special DK", Cypress

Pumpkin (DK, Light Worsted, #3)
Red Heart "Baby Hugs Light", Orangie
Red Heart "Fashion Soft", Kelly Green

Cabbage (DK, Light Worsted, #3)
Lion Brand "Baby Soft", Pistachio

Basket (Worsted, #4)
Lion Brand "Vanna's Choice", Honey

Watering Can (Worsted, #4)
Caron "Simply Soft", Sunshine
Caron "Simply Soft", Blue

Shovel (Worsted, #4)
Caron "Simply Soft", Autumn Red
Caron "Simply Soft", Heather Gray

Compost Bucket (Worsted, #4)
Caron "Simply Soft", Limelight
Caron "Simply Soft", Chocolate

Caterpillar (DK, Light Worsted, #3)
Premier "Deborah Norville Everyday Baby", Green
Stylecraft "Special DK", Sunshine
Red Heart "Fashion Soft", Black

Earthworm (DK, Light Worsted, #3)
Stylecraft "Special DK", Raspberry

Banana Slug (DK, Light Worsted, #3)
Red Heart "Baby Hugs Light", Sunny

Snail (DK, Light Worsted, #3)
Loops & Threads "Snuggly Wuggly", Cobalt
Stylecraft "Special DK", Walnut
Stylecraft "Special DK", Camel

Spider (DK, Light Worsted, #3)
Stylecraft "Special DK", Camel

Ladybug (DK, Light Worsted, #3)
Bergere de France "Barisienne", Vitelotte
Red Heart "Fashion Soft", Black

Bee (DK, Light Worsted, #3)
Stylecraft "Special DK", Saffron
Red Heart "Fashion Soft", Black
Red Heart "Baby Hugs Light", Shell

Other Books by Linda Wright

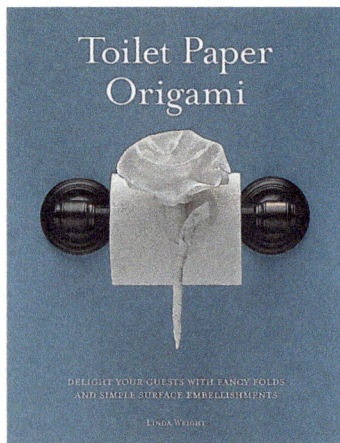

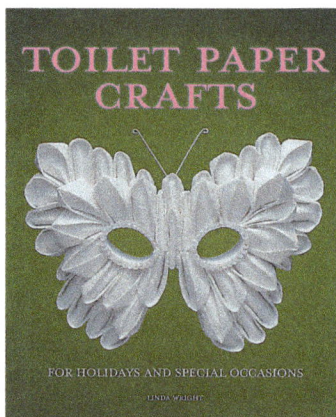

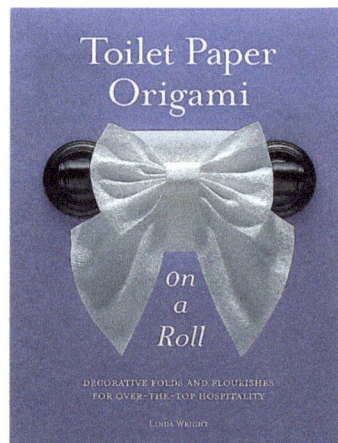

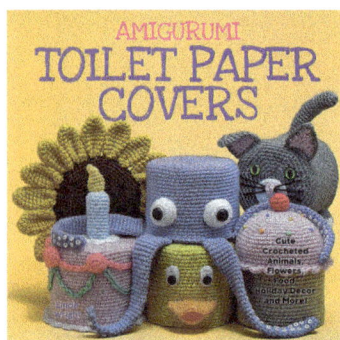

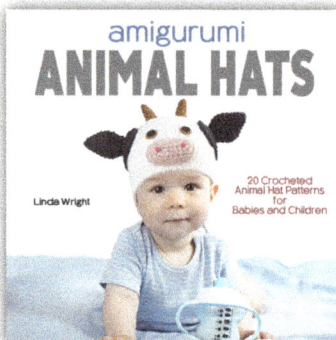

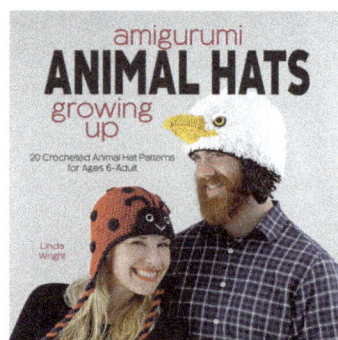

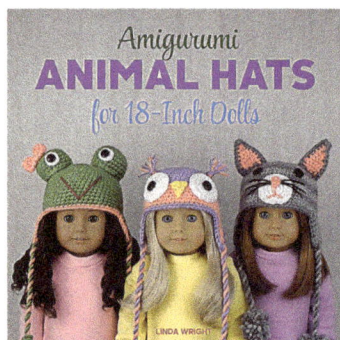

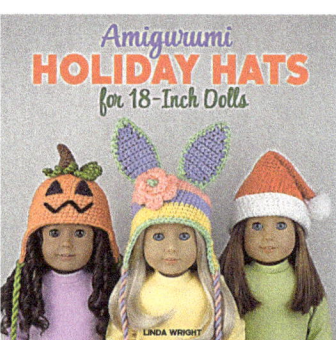

Toilet Paper Origami
DELIGHT YOUR GUESTS WITH FANCY FOLDS AND SIMPLE SURFACE EMBELLISHMENTS
LINDA WRIGHT

TOILET PAPER CRAFTS
FOR HOLIDAYS AND SPECIAL OCCASIONS
LINDA WRIGHT

Toilet Paper Origami
On a Roll
DECORATIVE FOLDS AND FLOURISHES FOR OVER-THE-TOP HOSPITALITY
LINDA WRIGHT

AMIGURUMI TOILET PAPER COVERS
Cute Crocheted Animals, Flowers, Food, Holiday Decor and More!

amigurumi ANIMAL HATS
Linda Wright
20 Crocheted Animal Hat Patterns for Babies and Children

amigurumi ANIMAL HATS growing up
20 Crocheted Animal Hat Patterns for Ages 6-Adult
Linda Wright

Amigurumi ANIMAL HATS for 18-Inch Dolls
LINDA WRIGHT

Amigurumi HOLIDAY HATS for 18-Inch Dolls
LINDA WRIGHT

amigurumi GOLF CLUB COVERS
25 Crochet Patterns for Animal Golf Club Covers
Linda Wright

LINDA WRIGHT studied textiles and clothing design at the Pennsylvania State University. She is the author of various handicraft books including the bestselling *Toilet Paper Origami* and its companion book, *Toilet Paper Origami On a Roll*; the innovative *Toilet Paper Crafts*; and numerous works of amigurumi-style crochet. To learn more about these fun-filled books, visit:

tporigami.com   pinterest.com/LindalooEnt   amazon.com/author/lindawright   lindaloo.com

Notes